Antranig Azhderian

Under Oriental Skies

Or, Asia Minor and her inhabitants

Antranig Azhderian

Under Oriental Skies
Or, Asia Minor and her inhabitants

ISBN/EAN: 9783744754736

Printed in Europe, USA, Canada, Australia, Japan

Cover: Foto ©Andreas Hilbeck / pixelio.de

More available books at **www.hansebooks.com**

Antranig Azhderian

Under Oriental Skies

—OR—

Asia Minor and Her Inhabitants

DESCRIPTIVE,

HISTORICAL AND PICTURESQUE

—BY—

ANTRANIG AZHDERIAN

CLEVELAND:
THE WILLIAMS PUBLISHING AND ELECTRIC COMPANY
1894

1894,
—BY—
ANTRANIG AZHDERIAN.

Half-tone Engravings by The National Photo Engraving Co.

To the
Memory of my Home
Across the Sea, this first-fruit of my
Youthful Pen is tenderly
Inscribed.

INTRODUCTORY.

BY REV. CYRUS S. BATES, D.D.

Mr. Antranig Azhderian, whom I have known for several years, and in whom I feel a lively interest, has asked me to write a brief account of his life, to be inserted in his book entitled, "Under Oriental Skies."

Antranig Azhderian was born September 1, 1871, in the City of Marsovan, Asia Minor. By birth he is an Armenian of noble parentage and ancestry. His grandfather, Simeon Azhderian, holds the honorable position of representative of the local Protestant community to the government.

Through the teaching of American missionaries, all the immediate relatives of Antranig became, many years ago, earnest supporters of Protestantism. His father and uncles were among the first adherents to the Protestant cause in Marsovan, and they are to-day among the leading members of the Church in that place. They are great friends to the missionaries. The Rev. Dr. Judson Smith, Senior Secretary of the American Board, in a recent letter to Antranig writes: "The evening which I spent at your home in Marsovan was a memorable occasion for me. I should like to send my kind regards to your father and uncles, in memory of the kind entertainment which they gave me six years ago."

After a course of several years in the common schools of Marsovan, Antranig entered Anatolia College in that city, where he studied for about four years. His vacations were spent in his father's store, or in travelling about the country. During his college days he developed a strong desire to visit America—a desire greatly increased by the fact that a young uncle of his, Garabed Azhderian, was in America, a student at Williams College. After a long correspondence between Antranig and his uncle at Williamstown, he was permitted by his father to journey to America, starting in the fall of 1889. On his way, in Constantinople, he become acquainted with the Patriarch of the Armenian National Church, and also with a number of professors in the Armenian and American educational institutions in Constantinople. While in Paris he made the acquaintance of a set of students from some American colleges, and visited the International Exposition in their company.

After a short visit to his uncle at Williamstown, Antranig went to St. Louis to become a salesman in a large Oriental store in that city. His ability and faithfulness in this position made so favorable an impression upon his employers that they sent him to Springfield, Ill., to take charge of a branch store, in which responsible and difficult work he was quite successful.

While in Springfield, Antranig made the acquaintance of the Rev. Dr. David S. Johnson, who became a very faithful counsellor, helper and friend. Through the influence of Dr. Johnson he entered again upon a course of study, being for some time a student of Blackburn University, of which Dr. Johnson was a trustee. The President of the college speaks of him as a bright and promising young man, in good standing, and enjoying the confidence and respect of the faculty and students.

From Blackburn University, Mr. Azhderian came to Ohio to further his studies, and while in college here he has been preparing and delivering lectures upon interesting themes on his native land. The lectures of Mr. Azhderian upon Oriental life and customs have been greatly enjoyed.

Baptized in infancy in the Armenian National Church, educated in early years in the Armenian public schools, and yet trained up in a strongly Protestant home, and spending his later years in America, he combines in rare degree sympathy with the old historic national and ecclesiastical life of his people with sympathy for western political ideas and religious thought. This double sympathy peculiarly fits him to interpret Armenian life and thought to us, thus giving especial interest and value to his lectures here. And when he returns to his own people, the same double sympathy must be of great advantage for the interpreting of our life and thought to them.

From what I know of Mr. Azhderian, I believe him to be painstaking, thorough and earnest in any work undertaken by him; and I anticipate for him a life abounding in good service to others.

Very sincerely,
C. S. BATES.

St. Paul's Rectory, Cleveland.

PREFACE.

The Oriental skies! far-famed and far sung, over-reaching every poet-land of mystery and dream! Heeding its wooing whisper, we leave the practical world behind, while our imaginations wing themselves on languid, listless winds, that know not cloud nor storm, save as recollection past.

They sing us on our flight the songs of the olden poets; they tell in sighing cadences the wondrous yearnings of heroic souls, who thought to know the infinite and solve the secrets which the blue depths well knew, but pityingly withheld. We journey to a land where faith is not a miracle, and where were nursed and suckled the infant religions of our world. Grown hoary with age, and wanderers far from home, they point with admonitions for remembrance to the land of their nativity, under oriental skies.

We wander back in time, and look upon the Son of Man, the Savior of the race, as he treads with holy feet the holy soil of Galilee. Back, back we go, to stand in purity and awe amid the lavished wealth of God, the paradise of love and flowers. We cannot go farther. And it is here, in this Eden of Armenia, whose beauty, blighted by the sin of centuries, still sings in tender tones, its lullaby over our race's cradle, we are, for the most part, to tarry with the reader.

THE AUTHOR.

CONTENTS.

I. Asia Minor.. 9
II. The Seven Churches of Asia.. 21
III. Armenia.. 49
IV. Armenia People.. 73
V. Armenian Literature.. 89
VI. The Armenian Church...102
VII. The Evangelical Church...118
VIII. Glimpses of Social Life..145
IX. The Turks...195
X. Taxation in Turkey..210
XI. Mohammedanism..217
XII. The Queen of the East..243

ILLUSTRATIONS.

Antranig Azhderian, the Author..............................Frontispiece.
Theatre in Ruins.. 10
Arch in Ruins... 12
Street of Knight Templars... 16
Towers of Fortress... 17
Temple of Diana.. 24
Gate of Stadius.. 27
The Aqueduct and Castle.. 28
Acropolis (General View).. 40
Temple of Cybele (two Columns)....................................... 41
Palace of Crœsus... 43
A Mountain Scene.. 59
Mount Ararat.. 62
Nature's Song.. 90
A Scene in Armenia.. 93
The Passing of Summer.. 96
An Armenian Bishop...103
Mgr. Khrimian, Catholicos of all Armenians.....................111
A Turk Grinder...148
"Sweetheart"..163
An Armenian Lady..170
A Caravan..181
A Freight Caravan..182
The Flock...185
Turkish Foot Soldiers..201
Sultan Amurath I. (Murad)..204
A Kurd...208
A Circassian...209
Moslem at Prayer...225
A Dervish...232
Dancing Dervishes..235
Constantinople—Panorama from Galata..........................244
Seven Towers of Constantinople......................................247
The Mosque of Suleyman and Golden Horn.....................252
The Mosque of Achmet (Ahmed).....................................253
Santa Sophia..255
Imperial Palace of Dolma-Baytche, on the Bosphorus......260
The Interior of St. Sophia..274

ASIA MINOR.

"We are now to tread upon a soil rich in interesting and splendid recollections."—*Malte-Brun*.

THE land of song and poetry, the blood-stained battle-ground of empires, the garden of Eden and the cradle of the human race—such is Asia Minor.

There, rising in distinct outline against the blue sky of the Orient is the snow-capped Ararat, the sole unbattered sign-board of the realms of the pre-historic. There, silent memorials of an eventful past, lie the ruins of magnificent temples and desecrated altars, inscribed indelibly with the impress of high civilization and successive religions, now dead forever. There, in short, stretches a country rendered by its eventful history the most interesting to mankind of any land, of any continent. Her position as a natural centre of three continents had a tremendous influence upon her commerce and civilization; and not only were her institutions thus affected by the surrounding world, but through her commerce she exerted a like influence upon others.

No region, save that of the Sphynx, offers such inviting opportunities to the lover of antiquarian lore. Amid her fair plains, deep valleys, mountain ranges and hills, where nature's gifts are so profusely bestowed, are strewn confused masses of temples, theaters, tombs, walls, columns, sculptures—memorials of people long overthrown and vanquished.

The dust of centuries is heaped over the site of her

THEATRE IN RUINS.

ruins, once the abode of "giants"—military, scientific, artistic, theological.

In this focus of continents, nation after nation, diverse and antagonistic in race and language, have crossed swords for the possession of the field—flourished and perished—each successive power leaving its indelible imprints and vestiges, from the mythical period of which blind Homer sings to the present era, when the slender minerets of Islam pierce the azure from every city and village.

Along the Helespont and the far-famed Mediterranean coasts of Asia Minor, Grecian monuments of intellectual and material progress are the most conspicuous. Hellenic art and science were not confined to the shores of Greece, but Asia Minor afforded an equally wide field for their development. There are paved thoroughfares; by the way-side can be measured the foundations of temples, theatres, arches, gymnasia and Cyclopean fortifications, indicating a state of opulent prosperity strangely mingled with an almost savage grandeur of physical endurance, and displaying all the vital elements of architectural perfection, with mathematical proportions of size, with harmony and symmetry, accompanied by fanciful ornamentations of sculpture and moulding which no nation has yet excelled or equaled.

Tombs still remain hewn out of solid rocks, some of polished white marble. The finest of those which could be removed now ornament the museums of Western Europe. A few, where kings were entombed, are twenty-five or thirty feet square, as large as some temples, and as highly ornamented in the style of sepulchral art, with war and hunting scenes, the figures of horses and the warriors, vigorous and spirited, and on projecting stones, life-like heads and paws of animals. Along the base are often found half-size human figures—all full of life and action. These scenes of war and hunting indicate the people's cherished pursuits, and perhaps suggest their continuance beyond the grave.

The ancient Grecian architects erected their temples on wet and low ground, perhaps to escape the convulsions of the earth; thus we find many temples buried below the

ARCH IN RUINS.

surface by the accretion of the soil. While retarding discovery, this has promoted preservation. What the wind would have coveted the worm has spared, and so some travellers have claimed that they beheld unearthed palaces and temples in a state of marvellous preservation, with the most minute and delicate sculptural details.

Numerous columns and friezes of beautiful sculpture that lay on every side as exhibitions of genius and prowess are gradually disappearing. Many have been carried away to Europe, and the rest have no meaning to the stupid mind and selfish consideration of the half-civilized nomads of Asia Minor, who have used them for. foundations, pavements, walls and grave-yards. Had the hand of man dealt as gently with this monument of skill as the tooth of time or the erosion of the elements, we could now visit temples, palaces and tombs, and find them as their artists left them at the last stroke of the chisel. Where earthquakes have thrown them down, they could be rebuilt from the fragments—their inscriptions and decorations sharp and distinct as when they were new. Such is the preserving character of the climatic influence in this region.

Yet not to the archæologist alone are the plains of Asia Minor rich and tempting. Here the botanist may revel in a flora, the most varied and the most exquisite in the world. Hither the glacier and the volcano, mepitic caves dead seas and buried rivers invite the probing. prying geologist. Here on the agate rocks of Phrygia, the subterranean streams of Lycus, the petrified cascades of Hierapotes, the extinct volcanoes of Laodicea, hitherto are drawn the energy and cupidity of Europe and America to the development of its wondrous natural resources, while the spade of the archæologist has been unearthing priceless treasures of antiquity. The diamond drill, with its almost endless cable, has often pierced the bowels of the native rock and caused it to vomit forth riches unsuspected by the natives who have lived and died above them for centuries, and the land of geography, the land made graphic by the pen of Herodotus and of Zenophon, is again the scene of numberless researches in topography and survey, whose object is the exploration of the world's fairest fields and noblest streams, that they may yield their tribute to Occidental capital and energy.

As we have intimated, Asia Minor is not only replete with monuments and relics, but rich in legend and historic record. Its ancient divisions, on the western coast Mysia, including the Greek colonies of Doris, Aeolis and Ionia, Pontus, Paphlagonia and Bithynia on the northern coast. On the southern coast Cicilia, Pisidia, Pamphylia and Lycia, with the inland provinces of Galatia, Cappadocia, Isauria, Lyconia and Phrygia, and more familiar to the modern reader than the department of France or the counties of England. They live in the pages of celebrated names, such as Ptolemy and Strabo. Strabo furnishes us with a specific knowledge, particularly of the central regions. Arrian narrates the marches of Alexander through the vast region of the Levant.†

Zenophon follows the road of Cyrus from Sardes in Lydia, passing through the cities of Phrygia and Lacaonia, terminating at Tarsus on the Cilician coast. Livy follows with the progress of Cm. Manlius. These interesting

---

† The modern name "Leavant" frequently used for Asia Minor, corresponds with the Greek term Anatolia, "Sunrise."

descriptions of old should prove of great value to the modern amateur in his researches.

On the borders of Bithynia and Mysia is Mount Olympus, her massive head rising 9,454 feet into the ether. This cloud-veiled summit represented the Grecian heaven, where the host of gods resided at the court of Zeus, surrounded by all the mythical conceptions of pomp and glory. But where are now the great family of gods? Are they dead? The summit of Mount Olympus is covered only with ice and snow, and they must needs have removed to more comfortable quarters. Not very far from this abode of lost gods, on the lake Ascania, is situated Nicaea, the city of Antagonius, whose possession has been vigorously contended during the medial ages between the powers of Turkey and Greece.

Amid all the associations and relics which crown her past, Nicaea calls forth from her bosom a hallowed reflection; for here was held the first Christian council, which Arostanes, a son of St. Gregory, and Archbishop Catholicos of Armenia attended, accompanied with King Trirdatis. There our Armenian royal and clerical dignitaries took prominent part in the Oecumenical Synod, and were entertained with much honor by the Emperor Constantine the Great. This first council originated the Nicaeno-Constantinopolitan Creed.

Along the coast of Asia Minor are many isles where cluster mythological legends, and where heroic grandeur and poetic enchantment reach the acme of perfection. On the southwestern coast of this region lies the island of Rhodes, her atmosphere so strikingly different from the rest of Asia Minor that it seems to be the combination of African and Asiatic zones; there pine and palm grow side by side; there is cloudless sunshine, salubrious air and

STREET OF KNIGHT TEMPLARS.

delightful climate, combined with the rich soil of evergreen gardens, blooming valleys, orchards of fig and orange trees, and all the endowments of nature are so charmingly attractive that the isle of Rhodes was a source of inspiration to the early Greeks in their numerous poetical legends. The creation of the island from the depths of the sea, by Helius, the god of the sun, and its many graphic descriptions, mingled with songs of valleys and mountains which abound in Grecian literature, can not fail to interest every æsthetic mind.

How inspiring to survey the deserted city of ancient

TOWERS OF FORTRESS.

renown, bearing the island's name! Its streets now quiet and lonely, its walls overthrown, the many half-obscured monuments, the castle and fortress of the Knights of St. John, speak aloud, amid the profound silence, of the eventful past. Art and arms, patriotism and learning, were the characteristics of this powerful maritime republic. There the eloquence of Demosthenes pleaded the cause of the city against the overwhelming power of Alexander of Macedon. There, astride the entrance of the harbor, the Clossus, a brazen statue of Helios, towers into the blue of the sky amid three thousand statues, as the wonder of the ancient world. Each isle, as each city of Asia Minor, possesses its own peculiar characteristic, and historical associations replete with war and romance.

Many toilsome tours and laborious excavations have been made in Asia Minor, many hardships have been patiently endured in the investigation of the ruins of the depopulated cities, and much is yet undone. Why have the intellects turned from the contemplation of realities to spend their precious hours wandering in the realms of dilapidated temples, theaters, tombs and old and mutilated inscriptions? Why? Do not these obsolete, time-worn relics furnish materials for the building up of modern scholarship? Is not the keen appreciation of the knowledge of the past the richest treasure of the intellect of to-day? (Investigations made in a land associated with such great names, awaken in thoughtful minds not only a scholarly interest but a peculiar fascination. This region was the birthplace of Herodotus, the father of Greek history, of Homer the poet, of Pythagoras the philosopher. Here lived Croesus, the patriarch of fortune and the patron of art).

From a scriptural view, the topography of Asia Minor is radiant with apocalyptic visions, and with apostolic labors, and with martyrs and missionaries of deathless fame. Every mountain and hill in Asia Minor will forever cherish the memory of St. Paul, the brave apostle of Christendom, against whom in vain have the furious armies of heathen opposition thundered. How inspiring to hear in the opulent cities of Greek and pagan Asia Minor, a voice most eloquent, the burning spirit of the great apostle of the Gentile world, pleading the Man of Galilee!

Asia Minor, the arena of diverse religions! where Christianity inaugurated its movement for universal empire, and where Judaism and Mohammedanism displayed their greatest exploits as religious institutions!

But where is the glory of twenty nations who on this soil once swayed a controlling influence? Where the seats of great military chieftains and empires contending for supremacy? Where the thriving commercial cities? Desolate! Graves of Homeric heroes are roamed over by sheep and oxen. Palaces of fame and wealth have passed away with their occupants. The throne of Antiochus and Mithridates have vanished as an illusion. No longer do the skies of Ionia smile on an enviable array of poets, who sang beneath her azure arch. The light of Asia Minor has grown dim! She is to-day a vast cemetery of entombed cities, destined to an eternity of desolation. Here and there are clusters of villages or a shepherd's hut, more like beehives than human dwellings, and a traveller, like Virgil's Libyan herdsman, carried with him bedding, weapons and all his wants.

As a bright day wanes and becomes lost in the blackness of a long, dreary night, the brilliance of Asia Minor is lost and long passed into the oblivion. For ages in the throes of political death, she yet declines to die. But the existing population, enslaved by superstition and ignorance, distracted by religious animosity and mutual jealousies, indicates but little hope of immediate improvement.

Nations, as individuals, are under the law and process of gradual development. The golden age of Pericles is but brass to-day. Centuries slowly, silently but continually, are marching on to higher, brighter attainments in civilization, learning and all spheres and activities of human life. Any nation and country, no matter what achievements crown her past, if irresponsive to the onward beckoning voice of the times, will surely be left behind. Onward or backward is the universal law of the ages. The ever-increasing aversions and antagonism between the population of the Orient and Occident shall continue until, by providential arrangement, Eastern ignorance and prejudices shall give place to the spirit of this advanced age, and Western ideas and methods become prevalent.

Oh that the trumpet blast of the nineteenth century would awaken those still in slumber! Would that this age of enlightenment might reflect a ray of light across the waters, where the riot of boundless superstition has for ages cast a gloom over the otherwise bright and peaceful world.

THE SEVEN CHURCHES OF ASIA.

AS the seven churches of Asia Minor are familiar to every student of the Apocalypse, a description of their ancient sites can not fail to be of interest to every intelligent mind, be he Christian or non-Christian.

Every year, numbers of travellers from all parts of Christendom visit these seven cities, because of their historic and biblical associations. Thomas Smith of Magdalen College, Oxford, is considered the first English traveller who visited the sites of the seven churches, and in 1676 he published, in Latin, a volume of great demand and interest, entitled, "Septem Asiæ Exclesiarum Notitia." Some, as Leake, Hamilton, and Arundell have turned their observations to account, and have given the Christian world much valuable information upon the subject. But most descriptions are extremely cursory, and because this is the case, and because we are from the land of those churches, we feel justified in presenting a chapter to our readers on this interesting topic.

A traveller seeking to inform himself as to the seven churches of Asia by personal observation, is apt to expect to find at least the ruins of an ancient edifice. So strong is this impression, that some writers have wittingly or ignorantly palmed off on credulous readers old castles or piles of stone as the very relics of Apocalyptic churches. The fact is, we have no evidence that any of those churches possessed a building, and if they did, no trace of them can be identified to-day.

The second and third chapters of the Book of Revelation are devoted to the epistles to the seven churches. These consist largely of commendations, warnings and prophecies:—commendations for meritorious labor and faithfulness, warnings against sins already existing or against future evils, and prophecies concerning the sure punishment that will follow the failure to profit by the given admonitions. As the traveller visits these old cities he can not fail to be impressed in the literal fulfillment of Apocalyptic prophecies, and as he stands amid the crumbling ruins that, as the dead camp fires, are left in the onward march of the triumphant kingdom, he is filled with hallowed emotions.

Let it not be forgotten, as we gaze upon the fragments of columns and cornices that were once parts of noble structures, that the admonitions and warnings originally directed to the seven churches may be applied with no less force and meaning to the churches of our day.

THE EPISTLE TO THE CHURCH OF EPHESUS.

REV. II, 1-7.

FIRST CHURCH.

Unto the angel of the Church of Ephesus write: These things saith He that holdeth the seven stars in His right hand, Who walketh in the midst of the seven golden candlesticks;

I know thy works, and thy labour, and thy patience, and how thou canst not bear with them which are evil; and thou hast tried them which say they are apostles, and are not, and hast found them liars:

And hast borne, and hast patience, and for My Name's sake hast labored and hast not fainted.

Nevertheless I have somewhat against thee, because thou hast left thy first love.

Remember therefore from whence thou art fallen, and repent, and do the first works; or else I will come unto thee quickly, and will remove thy candlestick out of his place, except thou repent.

But this thou hast, that thou hatest the deeds of the Nicolaitans, which I also hate.

He that hath an ear, let him hear what the Spirit saith unto the churches. To him that overcometh will I give to eat of the tree of life, which is in the midst of the Paradise of God.

EPHESUS.

The Temple of the Goddess Diana! The Temple of tradition and history, of song and poetry, that is what renders Ephesus great in the eyes of the modern traveler. But if you expect to see extensive remains of the great temple, you are disappointed. Time has dealt more harshly with this wonder of the world than with the Temple of the Sues at Baalbec. We must be content to look upon its ancient site and imagine it as it has been described by others, who, centuries ago, looked upon its beauty and grandeur.

But although description can afford us no adequate

conception of what the temple once was, yet a brief history might be interesting, as we contemplate the city so associated with its existence.

Going back nearly three thousand years to the founding of the city by Androclus, the last King of Athens, we find

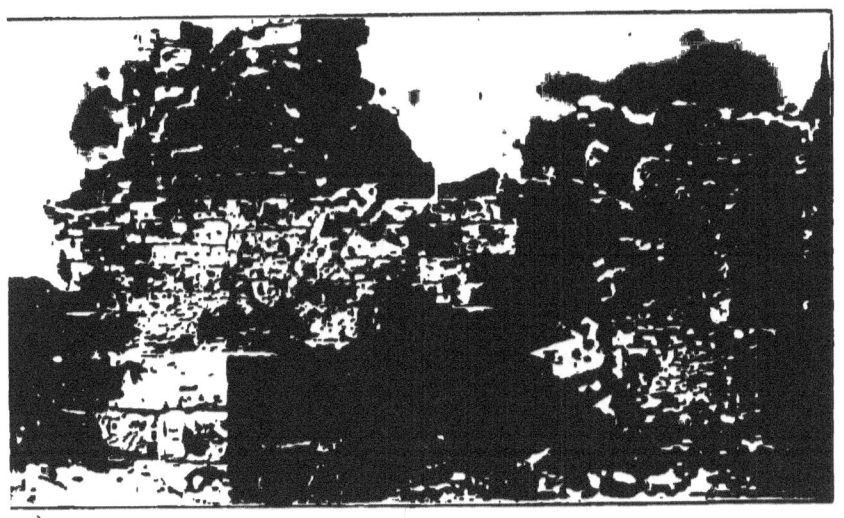

TEMPLE OF DIANA.

the first of six temples, which one after another were destroyed.

The great temple was founded in 541 B. C., and is associated with the number seven, not only in being one of the seven wonders of the world, but also as being the seventh temple erected on the same site to the Goddess

Diana. A very interesting tradition, which we would like to believe, tells us that a shepherd, caring for his flocks on the slopes of Mt. Prion, one day saw a fragment of stone rolling down the hillside, broken off above by the horn of a ram. Picking it up, he found it to be a piece of the finest marble, and this discovery gave to the builders plenty of the best material, close by, with which to construct the temple. Ctesiphon drew the plans, which, under the successive execution of famous artists and architects, consumed all of two centuries and a quarter, over seven generations, in erection. All Asia liberally contributed to its adornment. The entire structure was made of marble save the roof, which was of cedar, and the gates of finely carved cypress. The columns, we are told, were of one piece of fine Parian marble. One hundred and twenty-seven of these, each sixty feet high, were erected in the memory of as many kings, by whom they had been presented.

To form some idea of its vastness, let the reader remember that the great Parthenon at Athens was not one-fourth as large. The basement was so high as to require ten steps to ascend to the entrance. The aim of the architects and builders was not only beauty but durability, and as the ground of the site was very marshy, so selected because less liable to earthquakes, it became necessary to have a sound bedding upon which the foundation of so great an edifice might firmly rest. A concrete was accordingly formed of charcoal well rammed down with pieces of wool, which served the purpose.

On the sixth of Hecatomaboen (July) this wonder of the world was burned by Herostratus—an Ephesian fanatic, who sought to immortalize his name. On the same night, history tells us, occurred the birth of Alexander the Great, by which the magic of the time was greatly stirred, as they considered this occasion of his birth a sign of disastrous fortune to the world.

The temple was rebuilt in a far grander style than the former. Women poured in their jewels to adorn this sacred shrine. Its columns of jasper, its Ionic pillars of carved cypress-wood, painted by the most renowned of Greek artists, presented to the human eye a wonder of unsurpassed grandeur.

It seems incredible that time, unaided, can have so utterly destroyed this mass of material. We cannot believe it. Loads of marble have probably been carried away for residences, still more may have found its way to the new capitol of the Byzantine emperors, in compliance with their orders; perhaps some of the beautiful pillars to-day adorning St. Sophia, the admiration of the world, are fugitives from the temple that Alexander in ecstacy gazed upon; we do not know, but we do know that to-day not one stone of remembrance stands on the site once graced by the great temple of the Ephesians to the Goddess Diana.

The Gate of Stadium, the Aqueduct and Castle can easily be distinguished from other ruins.

The ancient Ephesus was situated in a valley, or, more properly, a wide and deep hollow. To the west is the sea, to the north the river Cayster, and on the eastern side are the fragments of a wall that ran southward over Mount Prion.

As we stand at the base of Prion and look upward at its precipitous cliffs, we observe openings which lead into vast artificial caverns in the mount. On one of them are the ruins

GATE OF STADIUM.

of an ancient Christian church, and here, it is said, are the sepulchers of St. John and Timothy.

The Christian traveller is filled with strange and deep emotions as he pauses here in a place hallowed by associations so sacred.

From the epistle of St. John it would seem that the

Ephesian, like some of the other churches, was troubled with a class of teachers or heretics called the "Nicolaitanes," for the spirit says: "But this thou hast, that thou hatest the deeds of the Nicolaitanes, which also I hate." The Christian church still exists, but the modern town has usurped the old, and the ancient landmarks are fast disappearing.

THE AQUEDUCT AND CASTLE.

Ephesus was always a great commercial city. Perhaps, owing to this fact, Paul made it the scene of his labors for three years, thinking such a center of heathen civilization a fit arena for the gospel. Here he consecrated Timothy bishop (1 Tim., i., 3), under whose co-operation the infant church grew and prospered.

THE EPISTLE TO THE CHURCH OF SMYRNA.
(REV. II. 8-11.)
SECOND CHURCH.

And unto the angel of the Church in Smyrna write: These things saith the first and the last, which was dead, and is alive;
I know thy works, and tribulation, and poverty (but thou art rich), and I know the blasphemy of them which say they are Jews, and are not, but are the synagogue of Satan.
Fear none of those things which thou shalt suffer: behold, the devil shall cast some of you into prison, that ye may be tried; and ye shall have tribulation ten days: be thou faithful unto death, and I will give thee a crown of life.
He that hath an ear, let him hear what the Spirit saith unto the churches. He that overcometh shall not be hurt of a second death.

SMYRNA.

There are two Smyrnas, the old and the new. Two and one-half miles from the present city, on the banks of the sacred Melest, the ruins of old Smyrna lie.

This city, though about ten times destroyed by fire and earthquake, has been rebuilt each time with surpassing splendor, and has always been a populous city and commercial centre of the Levant, and an ornament of Asia Minor from the Apostolic ages to the present day.

Here it was, according to tradition, that Homer was born, and the traveller is shown a cave, the very spot, so say the natives, where the father of poets composed his immortal lays. But since other cities of Asia Minor make similar claims, it is somewhat difficult to place any great credence in this assertion.

Old Smyrna is said to have been built by Thessus, an Amazon, and named after his wife, so accordingly the architecture of the place is called "Amazonian." Most of the city is built on the crest of a hill and probably so placed for purposes of defense. This view is further strengthened by the fact that the walls were made unusually substantial, some of the blocks being eight and ten feet in length. But two and one-half miles eastward, on the slopes of Mount Pagus, with its two miles of seacoast, is the new Smyrna of to-day, the largest and most important commercial city of all Asia Minor, the "Crown of Ionia," the ornament of Asia.

Tradition tells us that Alexander the Great, tired and weary with a day's hunt in the vicinity, went to sleep beneath a plane tree and dreamed a dream. In the vision Jupiter appeared and commanded him to build a city for the scattered Smyrnans on Mount Pagus. Accordingly a city was built on the summit of the hill, and the ruins of an ancient castle, said to have been built as a fortress by Alexander's generals, still remain.

Of more historic interest, however, especially to Christian investigators, is the immense stadium on a spur on Mt. Pagus. It was once a magnificent structure, but much of the marble, of which the seats were constructed, has been carried away by the Turks and used in building residences. It was in this stadium that the famous martyr Polycarp, "seed abounding," was burned (167 A. D.), and his example is considered such a means of edification that the story of his trial and heroic death is frequently read in the churches.

Three times was he asked to reproach Christ, but his

faith was not shaken, and he answered still firmly: "Eighty-six years have I served Him, and I will not forsake Him now." His tomb is still shown, designated by a fine old cypress tree.

Smyrna will ever be remembered for the life and death of this illustrious defender of the early Church. In the vast cemetery on the face of the hill, the great city of the dead is the glory of the Smyrna of old. Indeed, in our travels, as we gaze upon broken arches, marble fragments and monuments of memorial, we feel that Asia Minor is one vast, solemn cemetery of men and nations. "Westward the star of empire takes its way," and, as the dead ashes of watch-fires are left behind an advancing army, so nations in their westward march have left these traces of their visitations.

The city to-day extends from the foot of Mount Pagus, where the Turkish quarter is located, to the coast, where most of the European population lives. The Armenian portion is in the center of the city, and is the only portion where the streets are straight and wide. The Armenians form the wealthiest class in the city, and live in fine residences, usually built around an open court beautified by numerous shrubs and flowers.

The passerby can see and admire these courts through the hallways and corridors that open into the street, and sometimes (woe to our failing hearts) we catch a glimpse of an Armenian female, dressed in rich attire, gazing at us with those dark, lustrous eyes so common to the race. The streets in the Turkish quarter are very narrow and badly constructed, and, although the city looks quite picturesque from a distance, these dirty streets spoil one's first impression of the city's cleanness. At one time the residences were built of stone, but on account of the many destructive earthquakes, it has been found more economical to use wood. Smyrna is a city of considerable commercial importance, and on any week-day long lines of camels can be seen filing in and out of the city loaded with cotton, raisins, figs and fresh fruits. Indeed, Smyrna is the chief seaport in Asia Minor, and has the advantage of a good harbor, which, in ancient times, was said to be self-closing.

The Bezenstein, or market-place, is of considerable interest to the foreigner with its large stock of goods of all kinds.

Another place of interest is the Homerium, a library dedicated to Homer.

Smyrna has a population of over 200,000. Gas works, street cars and several railroads are the evidences of her prosperity. It contains twelve churches—three Greek, three Catholic, four Protestant and one Armenian. There are also four newspapers, one of which is Armenian.

From the fact that the city was the seat of one of the churches to which St. John was commanded to write, and because of its many historical and religious associations, the name of Smyrna will live on, long after the city itself has passed away.

THE EPISTLE TO THE CHURCH OF PERGAMOS.

REV. II. 12-17.

THIRD CHURCH.

And to the angel of the church in Pergamos write: These things saith he who hath the sharp sword with two edges:

I know thy works and where thou dwellest, even where Satan's seat is: and thou holdest fast my name, and hast not denied my faith, even in those days wherein Antipas was my faithful martyr, who was slain among you, where Satan dwelleth.

But I have few things against thee, because thou hast there them that hold the doctrine of Balaam, who taught Balak to cast a stumbling-block before the children of Israel, to eat things sacrificed unto idols, and to commit fornication.

So hast thou also them that hold the doctrine of the Nicolaitans, which thing I hate.

Repent; or else I will come unto thee quickly, and will fight against them with the sword of my mouth.

He that hath an ear, let him hear what the spirit saith unto the churches: To him that overcometh will I give to eat of the hidden manna, and will give him a white stone, and in the stone a new name written, which no man knoweth saving he that receiveth it.

PERGAMOS.

The valley in which Pergamos reposes is one of the most fertile in the world. The modern Pergamos, situated beneath a precipitous hill on the banks of the Caucus, occupies the same site as the ancient cities.

Third in importance in Asia Minor, Pergamos owes her prosperity to the commercial advantages afforded by her connection with the seaboard, twenty miles distant.

He who first mentions Pergamos in history is Xenophon. In his 'Anabasis' he tells us that Lysimides, a great general, built a castle and defences at the summit of the hill, back of the city, in which to hide his treasures. In later years this hill became the acropolis of Pergamos, and, to-day, the ruins of walls lie scattered about, whose architecture tells that they were erected by the Greeks many centuries ago.

Among other interesting remnants on the acropolis are the remains of a palace inhabited by various kings, for Pergamos was once the flourishing capital of the surrounding provinces. Eumenese, its greatest king, contributed much to the city's prosperity, presenting it with a valuable library of two hundred thousand volumes, which was the rival of Alexandria's in Egypt. With this library, Pergamos rapidly grew to be one of the most influential cities of the East, and, because of its culture, came to be known as the "Eastern Athens."

There are some walls still standing, near the river's edge, which some suppose to have formed the building which contained the library; but this is highly improbable, for its architecture would rather betray it to have been a Grecian church. Two towers rise on either side, in which it would seem stood altars devoted to the Grecian religion. In later years, this structure was converted into a Christian church, the "Church of St. John." Fragments of marble and pieces of Corinthian pillars lie all around this Basilica, but the marble is gradually being carried away for tombs in the neighboring Turkish graveyard.

To the antiquarian, Pergamos is filled with interesting relics. Very curious, to the general traveler, are the tunnels beneath the streets, and even houses, in which a great many people had their homes, as the Turk expresses it, "neither on earth nor in heaven." These tunnels are built so strong and durable that foundations of large buildings rested upon them.

A river flows through the center of the city, across which are thrown five massive bridges, marvels of art and beauty. Their history can be read in their architecture, for the main structure is Grecian and the repairs Roman, and by this alone it is easy to tell which had the later ascendency.

But most unique and ingenious was the amphitheater in the western part of the town, with a river flowing through its center, and so constructed as to be filled with water, no doubt for the display of aquatic spectacles.

What John writes concerning Pergamos is the most interesting of all the epistles to the churches. It speaks of "Antipas, my faithful martyr, who was slain among you where Satan dwelleth."

Tradition relates that Antipas was put to death in a horrible manner, namely, by being placed in a brazen bull and slowly roasted.

The city was famous also for her heathen temples dedicated to Zeus, Apollo, Athens, Jupiter, Minerva, Venus and Bacchus, all standing in a sacred grove. (Tacitus, "Annal," III., 63; Xenophon, "Arab," VII., 8-23.)

John also speaks of Pergamos as being the place "where Satan's seat is." Much of the religion of the

people of Pergamos was connected with impurity and
licentiousness, and the worship of Aesculepius prevailed
largely, to which John may have referred; but now, as
at that time, there are those that hold fast to Christianity, and the Church still flourishes.

THE EPISTLE OF THE CHURCH OF THYATIRA.

REV. II: 18-29.

FOURTH CHURCH.

And unto the angel of the church in Thyatira write: These things saith the Son of God, who hath his eyes like unto a flame of fire, and his feet are like fine brass:

I know thy works, and charity, and service, and faith, and thy patience, and thy works; and the last to be more than the first.

Nothwithstanding I have a few things against thee, because thou sufferest that woman Jezebel, which calleth herself a prophetess, to teach and seduce my servants to commit fornication, and to eat things sacrificed unto idols.

And I gave her space to repent of her fornication; and she repented not.

Behold, I will cast her into a bed, and them that commit adultery with her into great tribulation, except they repent of their deeds.

And I will kill her children with death; and all the churches shall know that I am He that searcheth the reins and hearts, and I will give unto every one of you according to your works.

But unto you I say, and unto the rest in Thyatira, as many as have not this doctrine, and which have not known the depths of Satan, as they speak; I will put upon you none other burden.

But that which ye have already, hold fast till I come.

And he that overcometh, and keepeth my works unto the end, to him will I give power over the nations:

And he shall rule them with a rod of iron; as vessels of a potter shall they be broken to shivers: even as I received of my father.

And I will give him the morning star.

He that hath an ear, let him hear what the Spirit saith unto the churches.

THYATIRA.

For a number of centuries the site of the ancient Thyatira was unknown. Much discussion has arisen concerning the matter, but now it is almost universally agreed that the modern Ak-Hissar, "the white castle," is the place.

If we look for ruins we are disappointed, for there are hardly any worth mentioning; in fact the city is the least interesting of all the seven, for here we see no ancient temples, no amphitheaters or crumbling palaces.

It is true that on the edge of the city a few fragments of pillars and friezes are scattered, but this is all there is to indicate the existence of the ancient Thyatira.

How can this be accounted for? Partly in the fact that the city is in a prosperous commercial center to-day, and as fast as commerce increases, relics disappear. That this has had something to do with it, there is no doubt.

Thyatira is situated in the north of Lydia, on the banks of the river Lycus. Near by is a solitary and desolate plain, the plain of Antiocus. Here was present in battle Antiochus the Great. Here also stood two commanders who had decided the fate of Rome and Carthage on the field of Zama, Scipio and Hannibal.

In this city there are nine mosques and one Greek church. No Christian church exists there to-day. There are also a few Greek and Armenian priests in Thyatira, which is under the ecclesiastical jurisdiction of the Bishop of Ephesus. About two or three hundred Armenians reside in Thyatira.

Probably it was the commerce in purple dye that brought the city in contact with Christianity, for when St. Paul was in Philippi, he says: "On the Sabbath day we went out by a river side where prayer was wont to be made and we sat down and spoke unto the women which resorted thither; a prophetess to seduce my servants to commit fornication and to eat things sacrificed unto idols."

The remains of the Apocalyptic Church cannot be identified. Some affirm that it stood near the Turkish cemetery, and that its ruins are among those of other edifices that form a mound close by. Others with as much confidence assert that its remains are to be found in the town, not far from the little Armenian church, where several broken columns lie. Perhaps neither site is the correct one.

Doubtless the religious impurities here mentioned in time destroyed all Christianity of a true nature, and to-day Thyatira has not one place where Christian worship is conducted.

THE EPISTLE TO THE CHURCH OF SARDIS.

REV. III., 1-6.

FIFTH CHURCH.

And unto the angel of the Church in Sardis write: These things saith he that have the seven Spirits of God, and the seven stars; I know thy works, that thou hast a name that thou livest, and art dead.

Be watchful, and strengthen the things which remain, that are ready to die; for I have not found thy works perfect before God.

THE SEVEN CHURCHES OF ASIA. 39

Remember, therefore, how thou hast received and heard, and hold fast, and repent. If therefore thou shalt not watch, I will come on thee as a thief, and thou shalt not know what hour I will come upon thee.

Thou hast a few names even in Sardis which have not defiled their garments; and they shall walk with me in white: for they are worthy.

He that overcometh, the same shall be clothed in white raiment; and I will not blot out his name out of the book of life, but I will confess his name before my Father, and before his angels.

He that hath an ear, let him hear what the Spirit saith unto the churches.

SARDIS.

Half way between Smyrna and Philadelphia, under the snow-capped Tmolus range, in the valley of Hermus river, the ruins of ancient Sardis lie.

If we climb to the summit of a rocky hill in the southern end of the town in the early morning, a little after sunrise, we will obtain an excellent view of the country about and the town beneath our feet.

We are standing on what was formerly the Acropolis. All around us are piles of stone that once composed a strong line of fortifications. Looking southward we see the snow-crowned peaks of the mountains.

Across the plain the river Hermus gradually widens as it seeks to lose itself in the sea. Beyond, glistening in the sunlight is Lake Gyges, so named after the traditional founder of the city, who is supposed to have lived about 718 B. C. Near the lake are seventy or eighty mounds, the graves of ancient kings, the Necropolis of Sardis.

In the centre of these mounds is one, higher than the others, built in honor of Alyates, a famous military king, who conquered all Asia Minor and placed it under his rule.

From a cleft in the mountain side, the classic stream Pactolus gushes forth and winds partially around the hill upon which we stand. It was on the bank of this stream that Sophocles pictures the Goddess Cybele, and on its bank are the ruins of a magnificent temple erected in her

ACROPOLIS (GENERAL VIEW).

name. This was the finest piece of architecture in Sardis. There are only two columns remaining to-day, and critics pronounce them the finest Ionic columns in existence. It is to be deplored that the temple of Sardis is not in a better state of preservation, that we might conceive something of

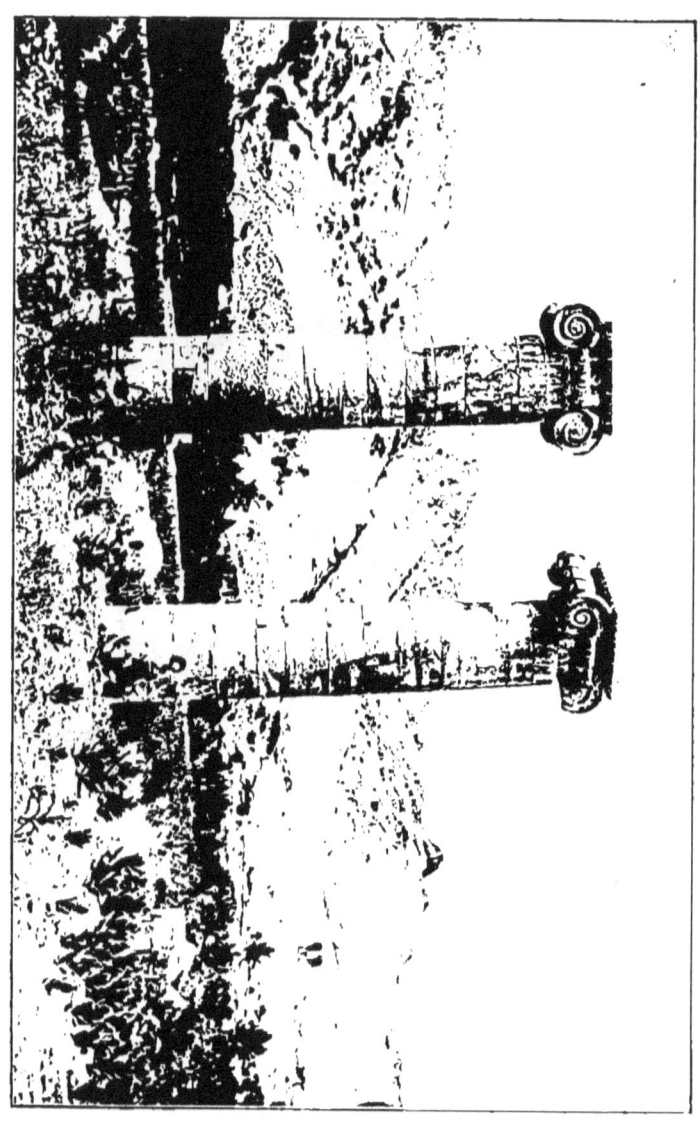

its former grandeur. Most of the marble that composed it has been carried away by the Turks.

At a turn in the river, parts of the wall that belonged to the famous palace of Croesus still stand. This palace or "Gerusia," a massive and impressive structure, was the residence of the wealthy Croesus of history. Two chambers still remain in perfect condition. The walls of this edifice, ten and one-half feet in thickness, were built of brick and faced with the finest marble.

As our eye scans the city, in the plains below we notice what were formerly the basements of buildings, rising above the ground. These basement walls were once many feet below the surface, and their present condition is due to the inundations and storms which have gradually washed away the ground about them.

Sardis is noted in history as a capitol of the ancient kingdom of Lydia, and also as a repository of the immense riches of Croesus.

The Lydians are supposed to have taught the world how to coin gold and silver.

When Sardis was at the height of prosperity, Solon walked among its magnificent buildings, and Xerxes made it the headquarters of his large army during the winter preceding his invasion of Greece.

It is not certainly known when or by whom Christianity was introduced into Sardis, although some claim that St. John preached there. It was to this church St. John was commanded to write: "Be watchful and strengthen the things which remain that are ready to die, for I have not found thy works perfect before God."

Historical Sardis is no more. Its churches have perished, and not so much as their ruins can be discovered to-day.

PALACE OF CROESUS.

Temples that were once the finest in the world have met destruction by earthquake and fire; the gorgeous palace of Croesus is the abode of the owl and the jackal, and the streets that once swarmed with a busy and prosperous population are to-day deserted.

THE EPISTLE TO THE CHURCH OF PHILADELPHIA.

REV. III, 7-15.

SIXTH CHURCH.

And to the angel of the church in Philadelphia write: These things saith he that is holy, he that is true, he that hath the key of David, he that openeth and no man shutteth; and shutteth, and no man openeth;

I know thy works: behold I have set before thee an open door, and no man can shut it: for thou hast a little strength, and hast kept my word and hast not denied my name.

Behold, I will make them of the synagogue of Satan, which say they are Jews, and are not, but do lie; behold, I will make them to come and worship before thy feet, and to know that I have loved thee.

Because thou hast kept the word of my patience, I also will keep thee from the hour of temptation, which shall come upon all the world, to try them that dwell upon the earth.

Behold, I come quickly: hold that fast which thou hast, that no man take thy crown.

Him that overcometh will I make a pillar in the temple of my God, and he shall go no more out: and I will write upon him the name of my God, and the name of the city of my God, which is New Jerusalem, which cometh down out of Heaven from my God: and I will write upon him my new name.

He that hath an ear, let him here what the Spirit saith unto the churches.

PHILADELPHIA.

Taking Smyrna as a starting point, and traveling eastward in the valley of Hermus, called by Homer on account of its beauty the "Asian Meadow," we reach the suburbs of Philadelphia, a distance of 68 miles from the seacoast.

The city, founded and named by Attalus Philadelphus, is beautifully located upon a plain at the foot of the Mount Tmolus range, near the southern bank of the river Cogamus.

The water of this river is peculiarly suited for dyeing purposes, and consequently the city is the resort of numbers of Armenian merchants.

The best view is obtained from the eastern slope of Mount Tmolus. There, at the outskirts of the city, extensive vineyards can be seen stretching away in the distance.

Massive walls once closed the city in a square, but are now in a ruined condition. With this exception, Philadelphia is almost entirely free from ruins of any sort, most of the buildings standing to-day having been erected in comparatively recent years. This can be accounted for by the fact that earthquakes are frequent and destructive, making it impossible for buildings to stand any great length of time.

One and one-half miles from the city wall, the traveller is shown a monument said to be erected of the bones of Christians who dared to resist the invading Turks about the year 1291. Whether or no this monument is made of Christian bones, it is true that the Philadelphian Christians have always proved themselves zealous in their religion, and have always defended their city from the depredations of invaders.

There are twenty-five so-called Christian churches, but services are confined to five of this number. What was once the most prosperous, the "Church of St. John," is now converted into a Turkish mosque, and the worship of God is supplanted by the Mohammedan faith.

The Philadelphian was the purest of all the seven churches when St. John wrote, and, considering the harassing invasions to which they have been subject, the people have well preserved their pristine purity of religion.

THE EPISTLE TO THE CHURCH OF LAODICEA.

REV. III., 14-22.

SEVENTH CHURCH.

And unto the angel of the Church of the Laodiceans write: These things saith the Amen, the faithful and true witness, the beginning of the creation of God:

I know thy works, that thou art neither cold nor hot; I would thou wert cold or hot.

So then because thou art lukewarm, and neither cold nor hot, I will spew thee out of my mouth.

Because thou sayest, I am rich, and increased with goods, and have need of nothing; and knowest not that thou art wretched, and miserable, and poor, and blind, and naked:

I counsel thee to buy of me gold tried in the fire, that thou mayest be rich; and white raiment, that thou mayest be clothed, and that the shame of thy nakedness do not appear; and anoint thine eyes with eyesalve, that thou mayest see.

As many as I love, I rebuke and chasten; be zealous therefore and repent. Behold I stand at the door, and knock: if any man hear my voice, and open the door, I will come in to him and will sup with him, and he with me.

To him that overcometh will I grant to sit with me in my throne, even as I also overcame, and am set down with my Father in his throne.

He that hath an ear, let him hear what the Spirit saith unto the churches.

LAODICEA.

One hundred and thirty miles southeast from Smyrna, in Asia Minor, on a cluster of seven small hills, lie the ruins of a once beautiful city. Of temples and theatres and a dense population of people, naught remains to-day save piles of broken marble and a solitary graveyard. "Desolation" seems to be the first word that suggests itself to the traveller.

The ruins of Laodicea, upon the sides of the lofty chain of Messogis, are three or four miles in circumference. At the north end is an old but massive stone bridge, from which a road leads to a three-arched entrance in the city wall, parts of which still remain.

An immense amphitheatre, finished by the Roman emperor about 86 A. D., still stands, and is in an excellent state of preservation. Ten years were consumed in the erection of this amphitheatre, which is one thousand feet square and capable of seating thirty thousand people. At the entrance, on the moulding, there are the remains of a Greek inscription. It is translated as follows:

> To the Emperor Titus Cæsar Augustus Vespasian, seven times Consul, son of the Emperor, the Governor Vespasian, and to the people—Nicostratus the younger, son of Lycias, son of Nicostratus, dedicated . . . at his own expense—Nicostratus . . . his heir, having completed what remained of the work, and Marcus Alpius Trajanus, the Pro-Consul, having consecrated it."

This inscription proves that this structure was constructed after St. John saw the vision on Patmos. A little north of the amphitheatre the remains of three theatres can be seen. One of them is four hundred and fifty feet in diameter.

There were at one time three Christian churches, but the ruins of them are in such a scattered condition that it is impossible to locate them with any certainty.

Truly the prophecy uttered in the third chapter of Revelation has been fulfilled in the entirety of the city's destruction. There is neither house nor mosque.

Laodicea was at the height of its prosperity about the beginning of the Christian era, when it conducted, despite its inland position, an extensive trade in wool. Soon Grecian art was introduced, and later a school of medicine was founded which became known world wide.

Its decline may be attributed to the fall of the Roman empire, although constant earthquakes occurring in the locality had much to do with its depopulation. No other of the seven cities shows the marks of the visitations of God as does Laodicea.

Smyrna, one hundred and thirty miles away, still stands and is inhabited to this day, but with the exception of a few who live in the empty tombs, Laodicea is the abode of none but the foxes and eagles of the country about.

The city has some historic interest, for two important councils of the early church were held here, one of which divided the scriptural canon from the Apocalypse, and here was the seat of a metropolitan. It is highly probable that it was the field of some of Paul's labors, although this is not yet established. The city is known to-day by the name Eskihissar, meaning "Old Castle." It was originally known as Diospolis, the "City of Great God."

ARMENIA.*

"It would be difficult to point out a more delightful, soul-inspiring mysteriously fascinating country on the surface of the globe than Armenia . . . Withersoever we turn our steps, to the north, south, east or west, the ground we tread is holy. It is history—stratified.—*E. H. B. Lanin, London, England.*

ARMENIA, now in the most part subservient to the Turkish Empire, is the fountain-head of antiquity. She is most ancient among the ancient—a land of awe and marvels. Her shrines, rocks, rivers, valleys and mountains —silent witnesses of pre-historic contentions and of changing fortunes—are replete with memorials which date back to the beginnings of the life and growth of infant humanity. The murmuring of her soft breezes wafts to the listening ear the sweet strains which once rose from the terrestrial paradise to mingle with the melodies of the celestial—a land where man first communed with his God!

In the earliest ages of the world, long before the nations and peoples of recorded history existed and flourished, the human race had its home in Armenia. Here was spoken a common language, here was a common monotheistic religion and civil government, and from here, when the race

*From a lecture delivered by the author in Y. M. C. A. Hall, Cleveland, Ohio, November 2, 1892.

grew and multiplied, were scattered her people over all Asia and Europe.

The position of Central Armenia, at the opening between the Caspian and Black Seas, facilitated the immediate extension of the post-diluvian people. Some writers on the Aryan controversy claim that the Hindookoosh mountains form the oldest home and distributing point. We contend that geographical position, Holy-writ, modern history, scientific research, archæology and tradition favor Armenia as the primitive home from which eastern and western Aryans originated. Mt. Ararat, where, according to the testimony of the scriptures, Noah's ark rested, is in the central province of Armenia. Some yet question whether the mountain of the flood is the Ararat of Armenia, and thus shift and drift the poor old ark from its restful abode, hither and thither—some to Mount Meiru of India, some to the Kurdish mountains of Central Asia.

What more decisive proof can we have of the diluvian narrative than the clear and precise topographical reference in the scriptures—Gen. viii., 4: "In the seventh month, on the seventeenth day of the month, the ark rested upon the mountains of Ararat." Remarkably harmonious are our indigenous traditions with Biblical document. There is a commemoration of the fact in the name of a village at the entrance to the glen on the northeast foot of Mount Ararat, called *Arghuri*, meaning "he planted the vine," where the Noah's vineyard is still pointed. In 1840 a tremendous catastrophy buried the oldest village and the vineyard; however, it is alleged that a vine stock planted by the patriarch's hand (Gen. iv., 2) still bears grapes. Not far from Arghuri is *Manard*, "the mother lies here," referring to the burial ground of Noah's wife. In a little distance is the city of *Eravan*, "visible," where the rescued righteous first beheld the dry land when the immense ocean of the ravaging waters subsided. Then the town *Nakchvan* "first habitation," indicating the primeval dwelling of man.

In these traditional spots the simple and credulous Christian of Armenia believes as manifest traces of the diluvian period. Mount Ararat is known among them as "masis," or "the mother of the world." It was also held by the ancient geographers that she was the center of the world. The Persian traditions, too, in regard to this mountain, are quite parallel with those of the Armenian. They call it *Kuhi-Nuh*, "the mountain of Noah." Thus not only have we the evidence of the Bible, but our traditions and the testimony of the old geographers are sufficient proof to sustain us in our belief that Armenia was the cradle of the human race.

Let me trace our country to still earlier periods. It was a prevailing view among the ancient Latin and Greek interpreters of the Bible, that after the flood, the human race, through righteous Noah, found a safe home in the very region which had sheltered its cradle. Surely the Divine wisdom had a lesson to teach the erring man, in restoring him the same abode from whence he has been once banished. And how wonderfully, again, does the topography of Eden, as given in the second chapter of Genesis, coincide with the natural characteristics of the region of to-day! Notwithstanding some obvious mixture of error in these traditions, undoubtedly they retain their bases in reality, with essential marks of truth. Streams of history, radiating from a common centre, have been transmitted from generation to generation, with some of the greatest events inscribed upon solid rocks, that the succeeding generations might not lose the thread of history. What had transpired prior to the deluge, one person, such as Lameck, the Son of Mathuselah, who lived from the days of father Adam to the second progenitor of mankind, would have been sufficient to communicate all particular events to Eber, Isaac and Levi, and from these patriarchs the thread must easily have followed to Moses himself. Should not the Armenians, who sprung from a remotest ancestry, rightfully suppose such a chain among their progenitors, which would justify their historical tradidions, especially in view of the harmony of the native traditions with the Bible. Again, we find various claims as to the location of the Garden of Eden. The latest and most absurd theory is its location at the North Pole, advocating that in the lapse of ages, the earth has gradually cooled off, consequently the first suitable place for man to live was at the Arctic Zone. What a habitable paradise would such a frigid region be! Our country, however, has the earliest and the most reasonable of all claims. Our land is the natural center. Where the Tigris, Euphrates and other rivers of the Paradise still flow, the identity of these streams alone should banish all doubt. The very odors of the forests are of singular fragrance. Indigenous plants of great variety and hue bloom here, which refuse to lend their beauty and ravishing odors to any foreign clime. Her numerous birds, too, with their many qualities, adorn and enliven the enchanting landscapes. Robert Curzon gives us a list of over one hundred and seventy kinds of birds in an Armenian city, ennumerating them one by one with their particular names and families. He says: "I have no power to do them justice. The number of various kinds of birds which breed on the great plain is so prodigious as to seem almost incredidible to those who have not seen them, as I often have, covering the earth for miles and miles, so completely that the color of the ground could not be seen." Do not all these natural and scenic characteristics, coupled with Biblical documents and native traditions, bear most circumstantial reminiscences of the primitive ages? Surely the Armenians are justified in their claim that the beautiful landscapes which were twice selected by the Omnipotent as the cradle of the human race, are in Armenia; that here was embowered the original Eden, and here the ark rested after the deluge. Armenians are thus ever proud of their land of fragrant memories. But what comfort can we obtain from a banished home! Paradise has been lost and transformed into a wild forest of fallen specimens of humanity, from whence her wisest decendants long removed to the remotest parts of the world. Some nations glory in their many past achievements and the monuments of antiquity; Rome, in her universal dominion, grand representatives, patriotism and statecraft; Greece, in her precious legacy of art and letters; Egypt, in her awe-inspiring ruins of ancient grandeur; Palestine, in her lofty sentiments of religious fervor, and Armenia in her prehistoric fame and the bloom of sacred memories. But may we consider all this past greatness worth much of itself? The Holy Land has left her Christ.

The dust of time and modern traffic has covered the exquisite monuments of Greek ideals and culture. They lie buried in ruins, and slumber mute and silent in the eternal death from whence there is no resurrection. All roads no longer lead to Rome, and the past is as dead in Armenia as elsewhere. It is the disposition of the nineteenth century to look forward to the glories of the future rather than to look backward to a glorious past. The palm and not the potato plant is the symbol of progress and enlightenment. Keep your roots in the ground and your fruits in the air, and let not the best part of you be buried. The richer soil your past may furnish you to flourish on, the better, but you must bear fruit in the present. Who are you to-day, as a nation or individual, is the question of the age. True, there is an inspiration for the patriotic heart in looking back upon the past glory of his mother country; and as I gaze upon the green hills, blooming valleys, venerable mountains, luxuriant pastures, rippling waters, the banks of the Tigris and Euphrates and the slope of Ararat, it thrills my heart with a deep pride in my native country. There our Armenian fathers bravely fought at the altar of civil and religious liberty—a land whose noble sons, the valiant soldiers of the cross, stood firm and pre-eminent for centuries against the sword and fire of avenging heathenism. Armenia! the mother of nations, the theatre of human and super-human prowess! the venerable shade of my departed fathers!

The genius of modern investigation was developed so far from the Armenian landscapes, that here, as the latest, is left the richest and most profitable field that can reward scholarship in every department of human knowledge. The geologist has yet to trace the changes that have created lakes where cities stood, or turned rivers from their courses. The botanist can here add to the world's knowledge of beautiful, useful and aromatic plants. Here philology has an ample field for the most acute intellect. The antiquarian can delve amid the ruins of cities that were great when Egypt was a new country. Ere Babylon was built, the men whose names these cities bore were fireside heroes in the most civilized regions on the globe.

Dr. George Smith of the British Museum, after an extensive exploration in the valley of the Euphrates, gathered tons of tablets covered with inscriptions, which he translated into English in a large volume, in which he carefully classified the facts thus collected. He places column beside column on the same page, one the Bible text and the other the text of the tablets, showing a marvellous agreement, thus verifying the statement that modern scientific research constantly corroborated the truth of the Bible. How happy do the periods of geological construction agree with the poetic account of the creation, as given in the Old Testament Scriptures. I am somewhat proud to think that my native land has been, and will ever be, a growing witness to the truth of the Mosaic record. Should the reader be disposed to doubt, let him read Smith's 'Chaldean Account of Genesis,' or, indeed, any of the modern works that treat of the wonderful revelations unfolded by the recent researches about the Tigris and Euphrates, Layard's 'Ninevah,' or Bishop Newman's 'Thrones and Palaces,' or the 'Records of the Past,' published by the authorities of the British Museum.

Because of the fact that Armenia's political existence has long ceased and passed under alien powers, I shall attempt but a brief description of her natural characteristics and history. Armenia, an inland region of Western Asia, like all lands of pre-historic renown, is a small country, a little larger than the state of Pennsylvania, and lies directly north of the Mesopotamian plain, between the Black and Caspian seas.

Her geographical boundaries, though constantly varied at different periods, extended to her largest limits under the administration of our kings, Aram and Tigranes II., to the Caucasus on the north, Asia Minor on the west, the Mesopotamia on the south, the Caspian sea and Media on the east.

In the earliest periods, our country was divided into Armenia Major and Armenia Minor. The former, known as Armenia proper, was divided into fifteen provinces, the central being the district of Ararat. The Armenian highlands are the most elevated mountainous region of Western Asia, consisting of a succession of rolling plateaux. Thus Armenia crowns the highest elevated region, with a mean altitude of from 5,000 to 7,000 feet above the level of the sea, and culminating with Mount Ararat, the loftiest in Western Asia, which forms the centre of the mountain system, with a vertical elevation of 17,210 feet above the level of the sea, or 10,210 feet above Araxes plain, above which she reposes.

The surface of the country is broken up by volcanoes and upheavals, and consists of a series of terraces, deep valleys, mountain masses and bleak plateaux. Here and there dislocation of rocks and mountains, and irregularity of the strata, afford convincing evidences of volcanic devastation.

From the Armenian plateau, at the front of Mount Ararat, arise the sources of the rivers of Western Asia. The Tigris, the Euphrates, the Aras or Araxes, the Cyrus (Kur), the Acampsis and the Halys, all have their sources within her limits and their estuaries in different seas. The two first, with deep and rapid waters, flow southeast into the Persian Gulf. The Acampsis (The Pison of the Bible by some), rising from southwest of Erxerum, fed and swollen by various streamlets, sweeps along with strong and smooth current into the Black Sea. Araxes (perhaps the

Gihon of the Bible) springing, about thirty miles south of Erzerum, from the side of Bingol or "Mountain of one thousand lakes," and with beautiful windings through regions of fertility and enchantment, mingles with the Cyrus, and both, with northward and again southward sweeps through the plain of Moghan, discharge east into the Caspian sea by three mouths, being navigable up to the point of junction. The name of the river, "Araxes," is supposed to commemorate Araxes, whose son was drowned in the rapid waters. Xenophon, however, traces its derivation to Ar-Ax or "holy water," which has been dedicated to the sun. This stream possessed different names at various periods, commemorative of various events. The Haly's or the modern Kizil-Irmak, is the most westerly. It springs from verdant spots, at no great distance from the Euphrates, and flows with rapid volume into the Black Sea.

The volcanic soil of the country is of astounding fertility and yields abundantly the crops of wheat, barley, apricots, maize, tobacco, rice and other minor products. Here is raised also mulberry, cotton, grapes and a dye called yellow berry. Beautiful vineyards, smiling gardens, orchards and groves abound in many parts of the country, especially in the valleys, where luxuriant vegetation would gladden the heart of the most critical epicurean. Productions of melon, fig, granate and trees of oak, pine, ash, walnut, apple, peach and chestnut abound. The land is also rich in corn and wine, honey, oil and olives.

Her wealth and boundless resources are even richer than the richest province of Asia Minor. There are gold mines on the line of communication between Erzerum and Trebizoud. The river Acampsis, the supposed Pison of the Bible, "which compasseth the whole land of Havilah, where

A MOUNTAIN SCENE.

there is gold," runs through that section of the country to-day. The mountains abound in treasures of silver, copper, iron, lead, antimony, sulphur and sulphate, especially in the west and amongst the hills of the Euphrates. Export minerals comprise salt from Lake Van, sulphur, iron and alum. There are stones of syenite, jasper, marble, granite and porphyry. Sand and limestones are the prevailing geological formation of the country, and are particularly famed, for from it our royal palaces and ecclesiastical edifices were erected.

The climate is healthy, and is varied according to the altitude of the highlands. The long winter extending from October to May is severe, while the summers are short and pleasant. The air is pure and delicious, the atmosphere clear and bright. Like all mountain regions, Armenia abounds in lakes. Among them Van, Sevan and Ormi or Orumiah are the most noteworthy. All lakes are petrified but Sevan, which is called "sweet lake." It reposes near the city of Erevan. Ormi lies in the southern part of the country, within the territory of the Shah's kingdom. Lake Van is by far the largest and most beautiful in entire Western Asia. It is embowered in the very centre of ancient Armenia, on the east of the city of Van, in a rich and verdant valley surrounded by green, forest-clad mountains. Its triangular surface is 5,000 feet above the sea level, with an area of 1,400 square miles. Its romantic beauty, the sluggish surge of its deep, blue waters, the fragrant associations, so famed in history and fiction, have been the inspiration of many a poet.

The petrified lakes of Armenia are particularly interesting. Such lakes are really the result of the evaporation of the sun's heat. During the warmest seasons of the year the water becomes crystalized like ice with deposits of salt an inch thick, which are gathered by the neighboring people into boats and carried away. In cold summers, the crust of salt on the surface does not appear.

Mineral springs, both cold and hot, abound. In my travels through the country I have seen many of them gush from the ground with great force from between the strata of limestone. These hot springs, so numerous, are another evidence of the subterranean commotion of the region.

People all over the country, who suffer any ailment repair to these waters, whose medicinal properties and chemical composition are of great reputation for their curative effects. Sometimes these waters are conducted to city bathing houses or basins by means of pipes.

As has been mentioned, Mount Ararat is the nucleus of the river and mountain systems, and is the center of the old world, situated midway between the Black and Caspian seas. It is a mountain rich with events of undying significance to mankind. Around its base legends and traditions, true and fabulous, hold perpetual carnival.

To-day it is the mighty boundary stone of three great empires—the Turkish, Russian and Persian. It has two summits, seven miles apart, the greater to the northwest extremity and the lesser toward the southeast. The snow-clad summit of the Greater Ararat is wrapped in clouds during most of the day. These float away at nightfall and leave the snowy crown clear and distinct against the starry sky. Seen from the northeast, a more rugged and awe-inspiring view is obtained than from any other point.

No one can do Ararat justice; every turn gives a new picture. Its beauty is considered unrivaled by any mountain on earth; it is truly "the sublimest object in nature." Its snow-crowned peaks, rising from the noble plain of

MOUNT ARARAT.

Araxes, rear in solemn majesty above the sea of vapor into the regions of eternal winter, perpetually covered with ice and snow. It is a picture of mingled sublimity and beauty, terror and tenderness—calm, cold, majestic—greatest in extent and loftiest in height! What an awe-inspiring sight, in the mellow radiance of the moon, to watch the changing hues and shadows of the venerable mountain, or to hear the thundering sound of falling ice and rocks from its stupendous dome! The snow-line on its summit, 14,000 feet, never dissolves and is one of the phenomenal features of this very phenomenal mountain, exceeding in quantity either the Alps or the Caucasus, as the former averages 9,000 feet and the latter from 10,000 to 12,000 feet in height of snow line. The surrounding people consider it a greater miracle to climb the summit; they believe the mountain still contains the relics of the ark, unchanged by time or decay, and in order to insure its preservation by a divine decree it has been made inaccessible to mortal approach. The Tartars and the Turks of the neighborhood imagine its summit the abode of the *Sheitan* "the devil" and wild ghosts, and they tremble to approach too near its top. Morier himself declares "no one appears to have reached the summit of Ararat since the flood." However, Dr. Friedrich Parrot of the University of Dorpat, after several unsuccessful attempts, finally gained the summit in September, 1829. He is considered the first mortal since the deluge who has ever ventured amidst the ice and snow of the isolated peak.

The name "Ararat" is of remotest antiquity. It has been known for 3,000 years. We find the name in the most ancient annals of Mosaic record of creation, "upon the mountains of Ararat." Moses of Clorene, the father of our history, affirms that the entire country of Armenia was known by that name, and he traces the origin of the word "Ararat" or "Arardhi" to our Armenian patriarch, Ara or Arai, the beautiful, who lived eighteen centuries before our era. At his fall in a bloody conflict, the Armenian plain was called after him, Arai-Arat, "the fall of Arai." Some others, as to the origin of the word Ararat, advance the theory that it was composed of "Ar" and "Arah," "Ar" in Sanskrit the "root of Aryan," or "nobles" and "Arah" "plains," or fields in classical Armenian, hence meaning "the plains of the Aryans" or "nobles."

The antiquity of the name Ararat antedates, a few centuries even the time of Moses. "An ancient bilingual tablet (W. A. I., II., 48, 13) makes Urdhu the equivalent of *Tilla*, of which the Accadian pronunciation is given as *Tilla*, the latter, as Sir H. Rawlinson long ago pointed out, being probably a Semitic loan word, and meaning 'the highlands.' *Tilla*, the equivalent of Urdhu, usually signifies the land of Accad or northwestern Babylonia, but since it is not glossed in this passage, and stands, moreover, between Akharru or Palestine, and Kutu Kurdistan, it would seem that it is here employed to denote Armenia. Urardhu, therefore, contracted into Urdhu, would have been the designation of the highland of Armenia among the Babylonians as early as the sixteenth and seventeenth centuries B. C."*

The term Ararat is used in the ancient annals of sacred

---
*"Cuneiform Inscriptions of Van" in "Journal R. A. S.," Volume XIV., page 392.

and secular history for the entire country of Armenia, and not for the mountain itself. Anciently, even the inhabitants or the modern Armenians were known as a people of 'Ararat.' It was not till of late years that the name "Ararat" came to be applied to the mountain itself. This misunderstanding has led some to erroneous conclusions and suppositions. Nothing could be more absurd to a native of Armenia than the idea that the ark rested on the very top of Mount Ararat. A well known American traveller, for instance, after describing his first impression of the mountain, goes on to say: "I could not help thinking what a hard time the mighty line of living things had when marching by twos, male and female, from those cold, bleak heights down into the plains below, after the great flood had subsided; and what a time good old Noah must have had to keep some of his warm-blooded pets from freezing on that lofty sixteen-thousand-feet-high pinnacle." A great deal of similar would-be criticisms have been made concerning the ark on Mount Ararat, as though that historic craft had presumed to rest on the very peak of the snow-capped pinnacle of symmetrical form. Such absurd criticisms, based upon false suppositions, indicate a lack of not only knowledge, but of a proper and common-sense understanding of the simple Biblical narrative. The geographical unit is the mountain range. With the mountain ranges the study of geography should begin. From them a scientific nomenclature can most easily be constructed. How precise and clear is the statement of the Holy Book, as inserted in Genesis "the ark rested upon the mountains of Ararat," and not upon Mount Ararat. There are Scriptural references in II Kings, XIX, 37; Isaiah XXXVII, 38. In these parallel passages allusion is made to Adrammelech and Sharezer, whom, having assassinated their father Sennacherib, escaped "into the land of Ararat." The prophet Jeremiah (in Jeremiah II, 27), summoning the nations for the overthrow of Babylon, calls "together against her (Babylon) the kingdoms of Ararat, Minni and Ashchenaz.

Thus sacred and secular writers concur in speaking of not only a mountain, but of a *range*, a *land*, a *kingdom*, an *army* and a *people* of "Ararat." Does our critic suppose that the horses and mules of Ararat were reared on the icebergs of an isolated peak? They were seen in the markets of Syria. Had they wings that they could fly where a donkey could not climb? An army of Araratians helped Cyrus in the overthrow of Babylon. Did they come on a toboggan slide from the regions of everlasting snow?

Moses of Chorene's appellation, "Arred," or Ayrarad, coincides with the Armaniya or Armenia of the Parsian text, which is frequently employed in ancient historical documents, denoting that the name Ararat was identical with the whole country of Armenia. St. Jerome himself always identified Ararat with the plain of Araxes, where the mountain reposes.

Again, the window of the Ark is described in Genesis as being above, and when "on the first day of the tenth month the tops of the mountains came forth," Noah would most naturally have been lower down to see what was above the Ark. Therefore the extreme cone, the highest pinnacle of Ararat, was not the resting-place of the diluvian ark, but in all probability a much lower part of the Ararat range.

In Armenia are many once famous cities unknown to Americans, because the hand of time has shorn them of their former splendor, and many have receded into oblivion, buried beneath the accumulations of centuries. The most and largest of them were situated on the fair banks of the Tigris, and comparatively few on the Euphrates. Some cities had their streets paved with fragments of sculpture when Moses was with Pharaoh on the throne of Egypt.

Fortifications in Armenian cities are numerous. Some of the walls still remain thirty or forty feet high, with solid stone foundations, and of considerable thickness. Towers rise at regular intervals, with large arched gateways. Let us recall some of the cities.

Ani, the city of the kings, the glittering city of gold and silver, was the imperial pride of Armenian sovereigns, whose pearly palaces in her gala days shone in the dazzling glare of the sunlight with beauty. Her streets were clean and richly adorned with lovely decorations of nature and art. This ideal city is to-day a heap of colossal ruins.

The venerable city of Van, anciently Semiramis city, embowered by the eastern banks of the lake, command a view of her wondrous citadel, towering on a rugged rock with a natural amphitheatre surrounding it, buried amid the loveliest vegetation and vineyards, presenting a picturesque situation that is beautiful beyond description or power to conceive.

Queen Semiramus of Assyria, with the exquisite taste of a woman, chose this paradise-like spot for her summer resort. On such an immense scale are the proportions of the buildings that it required six hundred architects and one thousand two hundred workmen. It was not alone the love of nature that attracted the queen to the vernal banks of the lake, but Ara, a young Armenian sovereign, who was famed throughout all the east for his beauty. Among many, Queen Semiramis was the chief victim of a love-stricken fever. In vain were all her charming manners, loving words and entreaties to the fair young Armenian patriarch, for he had rabidly denied with a shiver to be bound in sacred ties of marriage with an idolatrous ruler, who worshipped not the true God of his fathers. The exquisite melody of the nightingale, or the gentle swish of purling waters of the lake were mute to her; the beaming moon or gleaming stars had lost all spell and charm beside the charm of him who was the fairest of mortals. Even at night in her profoundest repose she was tortured with unrest. Shall her love consume her? She had determined to gain him—if not by will, at least by force of arms. How mysteriously strange is the path of love! She advanced upon the Armenian forces, but with bitter results, the clash of her conquering arms resounds, for Ara was sacrificed! It must have been a most tragic sight of wild despair when the stricken patriarch was laid low at the queen's feet, with the stamp of death upon his beautiful features. In vain were all endeavors of magic art to bring him to life. The spot where he was buried in a coffin of gold is still pointed out as "Ara Seni," "Ara is sacrificed."

The cuneiform inscriptions of Van are famous in history, as they have revealed the secrets of centuries and yielded up much to modern science. Prof. A. H. Sayce of Oxford, England, in his Journal renders the translations of these venerable inscriptions along with other researches of the Armenian antiquities, thus revealing the fact that the clear stream of knowledge has descended through succeeding generations to our day.

Artaxata, once the mighty capital of Amenia, where King Tiridates received his crown from Rome. After seeking for years to stifle the incipient church, he too bowed before the cross of Christ, and, like Saul of Tarsus, became the ardent advocate of what he once endeavored to overthrow.

The holy city of Vagharshabad was built by King Erovant, but all its pomp and glory have faded away, except the monastry of Etchmiadzin. This most ancient Episcopal seat of the Armenians still remains as a mighty bulwark, against which in vain have the heathen cannon of all ages thundered. This mother church of Ararat contains a number of holy relics, among them the head of the spear by which the side of the Savior was wounded, the hand of St. Gregory, the founder of the monastry, who laid the first stone in the year 302, that blessed hand that had baptized his haughty cousin, King Tiridates, by whom he had suffered unimaginable persecutions, and other saintly and hallowed relics which are kissed with devout reverence and awe. Our country being the first to have a Christian ruler, the traditions in this Episcopal seat are also rich in Apostolic legends. None of them are more singular than the reputed correspondence of Christ with our King Abgarus of Edessa. The messengers of this sovereign, having some business transaction with the Roman nobility in Palestine, heard of the miracles of Jesus of Nazareth, and on their return related them to their sovereign, who was convinced that either Jesus was "that Christ," or else God had come down to dwell on earth. As the King was suffering from a serious disease, he sent a letter to Christ with a company of messengers imploring Him to repair to his court and graciously cure him. At his request an artist was also sent so that if the Lord would fail to come, he would at least have his portrait. The painter being at work one day endeavoring to fulfill his royal commission, was observed by the Savior, who, passing a handkerchief over his countenance handed it to the artist with a perfect likeness of himself upon it. Duly an answer to the King's letter was written by St. Thomas, with a word of praise of his faith in an unseen Christ, and informing him that the Divine Master's mission was more urgent elsewhere than in Armenia, but that after His ascension disciples would be sent to enlighten the King's people and cure him from his sufferings. It has been stated that a papyrus has been discovered in an Egyptian tomb containing the reputed letter of our King.

Erzerum, on the main line of communication between Persia and the Euxine, still survives as a populous military post and commercial entrepot. She reposes in a lovely district about one hundred miles southeast of Trebizond.

By those who dwell in the vicinity, the city is thought to be the very spot where the Garden of Eden was located. They claim that for many a century the flowers of Paradise bloomed around the source of the Euphrates. Tradition says, nature herself was so horrified at the sacreligious conduct of a Persian king, that she refused to produce those rare beauties any longer, and even changed the course of the river itself. Local accounts of Adam's fall show how a frail, sympathetic man will follow a woman into any kind of a trap. He did not eat of the fruit, they say, until he saw its fatal effect on lovely Eve. Then, concluding that the Creator would have compassion if he saw them both in the same sad plight, and restore them to their former estate, he decided to follow her example. Reasoning thus, he indulged. We know the result! Restoration did not occur in accordance with his logical reasoning. There was something wrong with the premises. Logic was not taught, except objectively, in his day. Who can blame Adam? "The Lord cursed the serpent, and Eve and I were doomed between the two," was the sad refrain.

The extent of the fortifications is so great in Erzerum that they require 22,000 men to defend it. In 415 A.

D., the city was fortified by Antolius, and became a stronghold of the Roman Empire, and her ancient name, Karin, in honor of the Emperor, was changed to Theodosiopolis. During the early decade of the middle ages, she was an object of jealousy and contention between the Moslems and the Greeks.

There are also Armavir, Ardashed, Kemak and other cities, whose past associations are so fragrant and inspiring to an Armenian, while their present state is a little more than the shadow of their former grandeur.

ARMENIAN PEOPLE.

"Their national character is a powerful one, and will exercise a marked influence in determining the future of the East."—*Prof. Henry F. Tozer, Exeter College, Oxford, Eng.*

SINCE the tragic fall of Armenia, about the middle of the fifth century, our people, deprived of their heritage, have been widely scattered in all parts of Asia Minor, Russia and Persia, leaving but a remnant of the Armenians in Armenia. Thus when we speak of Armenians we must not be confined to Armenia alone.

The beginning of our national history, like that of all nations of antiquity, is mingled with much of myth and legend. Our father, according to our tradition, was Togarmah, the son of Gomer, who was the son of Japheth of the Scriptures (Genesis x., 3). Some of our historians allude to our country as *Askhanzean*, certainly derived from *Askenaz*, the brother of Togarmah and the son of Gomer.

Our traditional history dates from twenty-three centuries B. C., when Haig, the son of Togarmah, begins his political career as our first ruler, from which the appellation Haig, our national name, is derived. He was one of the many who were busily engaged in the Plain of Shinar in the construction of "The Tower of Babel," but the insatiable ambition of Belus, who sought supremacy, constrained Haig to flee from Babylon to the land of Ararat, where he proposed to plant his own dominion in the vicinity of Lake Van. Belus, the sovereign of Assyria, sending messengers to Haig, demanded him to surrender his power and return under his subjection. This haughty demand was promptly refused, and war was the consequence.

Belus, at the head of a mighty army, marched to the land of Ararat, and Haig met him with his patriarchal force of numerous sons, grand-sons and servants. It was a crisis which decided the future of his posterity. There the first Armenian hero displayed his valor and our legendary songs still sing his triumphant praise. He slew Belus with his dart and buried him on the spot where he fell, scattering his army in great confusion. Haig lived the long life of four hundred years, with a flourishing dominion. The first dynasty bearing his name had fifty-nine kings, with the capital at Armavir, to the north of Araxes. Here grew sacred forests, the rustle of whose leaves was held to be the voice of gods whispering to men of welfare and peace.

Haig's son, Armenag, was the next sovereign. Some suppose that Armenia derived her name from him. His reign is followed by a dim period in the annals of our country, which mention a succession of Armenian princes, until Aram, the seventh dynasty of Haig, comes to light about two thousand years B. C. From Aram, according to the best authorities, originated our present name, Armenia, by which we are known among foreigners. We do not use this name in our own tongue.

Aram was a king of unusual attainments, and a man of superior tact. He ruled the people with the power of a rightous judge and a promp executive. Contemporary with the Biblical patriarchs, he diffused his reputation far and wide throughout the neighboring provinces and countries, extending the boundaries of his kingdom by conquering large portions of Asia Minor and driving out the Median and Babylonian invaders. Among the few cities that he builded, Mazaca or the modern Cæsarea in Cappadocia, is the principal monument. His activities were cut short by death during the war against the queen of Assyria, after which Armenia became a tributary province to that country. The Haikian dynasty did not cease to rule, but it was reduced to almost insignificance beneath the mighty power of the Assyrian empire.

In ancient accounts Tiglath-Pileser speaks of "the mountains of Aruma," while the inscriptions of Shalmaneser mentions "The royal city of Arrame of the land of Unardhians."

This "Aruma" of the *Tiglath-Pilesar* and "Arrame" of Shalmaneser coincide with the name "Aram" of the Armenian historians. Different spellings of the same name account for its varied transformations into the foreign languages, while they both refer to the "Aram" of the natives, the first referring to the country and the latter to the sovereign. The derivation, Togarmah, is believed by some scholars to be from *Toka*, the Sanskrit for "race," and Armah of the classical Armenian, thus Aram, Arama, Arrame and Armah, though differently spelled by different people, are all derived from Aram, the name of the ruler and his province. Anciently the country was known as Aramenia, but now the name is contracted into Armenia.

The cuneiform inscriptions of Armenia are of great historical importance because of the light which they throw on the period between 856 and 640 B. C., but with this light is the shadow of religious and social Assyrianism throughout the southern and greater part of the realm. The Haikian monotheistic dynasty, though not extinguished, was almost eclipsed by the Armeno-Assyrian dynasty, founded by Lutipris after the defeat of Arame, king of the Araratians. This new and powerful line of kings continued from father to son in the following order: Lutipris, Sarduris I., Ispuinis, Menuas, Argistis, Sarduris II.

The Ursa and Argistis II., whose paternity seems undetermined, were evidently of the same family. Argistis II. was succeeded in direct line by his son Erimenas, and he by Rusas. Then last came Sarduris III., whose parentage is also uncertain. This era may appropriately be called the "Dark Ages of Armenia."

Its meager history, like that of Assyria, is engraven in cuneiform on monuments distributed throughout the region.

The inscriptions of these kings are of the vain-glorious, self-praise order, so characteristic of Asiatics.

Besides those of the local rulers, there are inscriptions at the city of Van to the god Armazt, or Ormazd, left by Xerxes, praising himself and referring to his father Darius. Curses of the air and sun gods are commonly called down on him who should dare to mar these inscriptions. However, some of the stones thus inscribed are now found in the walls of Christian churches with the continuity of their record broken. In some other cases they are still legible. Though religion, manners and customs in the region of Ararat during this era were Assyrian, and though their inscriptions were cuneiform, still the Armenians had a language of their own in which they shielded their identity.

Through a multitude of the fortunes of war, they have emerged from the retreating files of conflicting armies a national unit. They have furnished the battlefield for Assyrians, Greeks, Persians, Scythians, Romans, Medo-Persians, Saracens, Turks and Kurds. The evidence of history overwhelmingly affirms that, through it all, no material amalgamation with the invaders has ever occurred. This exceptional result, as compared with other less fortunate nations, must be attributed first of all to the reverence for "home," its domestic ties and sacred obligations. The social law and customs preventing the intermarriage of relatives has done much to sustain the physical health, which the fine climate of our mountain homes and rural life for ages engendered.

For centuries prior to the introduction of Christianity, Armenia was practically divided into eastern and western Armenia, or Armenia Major and Armenia Minor, the former east of the Euphrates river and the latter west of it.

Tigranes I., a king of Armenia, was the friend and colleague of Cyrus, and aided him in the overthrow of Babylon in fulfillment of prophesy (Jeremiah ii., 27-28). His descendants possessed the land of their ancestor in comparative peace, until Alexander the Great invaded Armenia (328 B. C.).

Before the long spears, splendid discipline and unquestioned bravery of the Macedonian Phalanxes, king Vahi of Armenia fell in defence of his country and people. His memory is embalmed in the songs and legends of our countrymen.

In 217 B. C. Macedonian rule ceased, and the country (Armenia Major) became independent, and this state of affairs continued until the death of Ardvates our king, thirty-three years later, when we submitted to Syria. About 190 B. C., Artaxias proclaimed Armenia Major independent, and offered an asylum to Hannibal, the greatest strategist of all times. who had sworn to his father, when a boy of twelve years, "eternal enmity to Rome," and for forty years had kept the field against the Imperial Eagles. It must have required courage of the highest order to harbor the greatest enemy of Rome. Lesser Armenia soon followed the example of Greater Armenia and revolted under Zadriades, whose descendants kept the throne until the time of Tigranees II., when it became part of Greater Armenia.

About the middle of the second century, B. C., the mighty hand of Mithridates, the Parthian king, laid hold of Amenian affairs and placed his brother Valarsaces on the throne. Under his rule the country flourished, laws were established, personal merit among his subjects was rewarded, and great cities founded. His wise policy laid a good foundation for a great empire. The superior talents of his great-grandson, Tigranes, had nearly accomplished this result, when the advice of his father-in-law, Mithridates of Pontus, brought him in conflict with the Roman empire, and opened the way for that widespread influence of Rome, which was to prepare the way for the kingdom of peace in the hearts of men, soon to be proclaimed to the world.

By a compromise all of Armenia except two provinces, Sophene and Gordyene, became Roman provinces. What was left became the Kingdom of Tigranes. Tigranes himself ruled the Roman Armenian provinces as a loyal Roman governor, until the time of his death (55 B. C.), and in this office was succeeded by his son, Artavasdes. The true greatness of the father was not inherited by the son, who violated his obligations to Rome, was arrested by Mark Antony, carried away as prisoner, and beheaded by Cleopatra, whose charms had captured Antony in Egypt (30 B. C.).

A son of Artavasdes, aided by the Parthians, in a rebellion which followed this event, massacred all the Romans found in Armenia. The Armenians looked to the Parthians as their natural allies, while the events of history prove that it would have been wiser to have followed the policy of great Tigranes I. and remained loyal to Rome.

The massacre of the Romans was followed by a period of anarchy, which is one of the darkest pages in Armenian history, as it was the legitimate result of the violation of solemn pledges; at any rate, poor Armenia was between two mill-stones, Rome on the west and Parthia on the east. The latter was desperate in the throes of declining power, with Persia crowding hard for supremacy in the region of Ararat. Within his own borders, too, Armenia was torn by the broils of a multitude of claimants who were struggling for the throne. In the midst of this domestic strife, an alien usurper, Erovant, became a sort of king (58 A. D.) and kept in power until his overthrow by Ardashes, one of the Arsacidæ line, Ardashes, who did some good for his people, though several times dethroned by the power east and west of his country. In 232 A. D. the Armenians became subject to Persia, through the attempt of their king, Chosroes the Great, to retain the Arsacidæ in power. With the assassination of the Armenian king begins one of the most remarkable chapters in all history. The deed was done, it is claimed, by the father of St. Gregory, the Christian illuminator of Armenia.

All of the royal family except Tiridates, who escaped to

Rome, was slain. In return the assassin and his entire family except Gregory, who was then two years old and was saved by a nurse, were slain.

Tiridates made an alliance at Rome, taking upon himself the obligations of Tigranes the Great—which were broken by Tigranes' son, to the sad undoing of Armenia for three hundred years. He was rewarded by Rome with the throne of his unhappy country. His honorable course was approved of heaven, in that he became the first Christian sovereign. In the first acts of his reign he persecuted the Christians, but like Paul he verily believed that he was right in doing so. Gregory, the son of the assassin of his father, received a Christian education at Cesarea and at Rome. He went to preach the Gospel in his native Armenia, but the king imprisoned him for fourteen years in a dungeon. The light of truth could not be imprisoned, and beginning with the king and the nobles it soon won the hearts of nearly all the people.*

This religious change angered the Persians, so that the political troubles continued until Theodisus the Great ceded the eastern part of the country to Persia, which was then called Perse-Armedia. Here we have Persian and Roman Armenia, governed by native rulers of the Armenian family until 652 A. D. During this period the Persians were untiring in their efforts to do Christianity. Among the Armenians numerous insurrections resulted, the

* The history of the Armenian church will be found in an appropriate chapter bearing on that subject.

most remarkable of which was led by Vartan Mamigonian. Bishops and priests were massacred at once, or carried away to give up their lives in Persia. The fate of the women is not recorded, but may be imagined. Christian schools and churches were razed to the ground.

In the recesses of the mountains the Christian Armenians still had their way until 485 A. D., when another conflict with the Persians under Prince Vahan occurred. In these religious battles the slaughter of the Persians was so great that a compromise granting the Christians religious liberty was effected. From this time to 632 our unhappy lot, owing to many petty strifes, was less intolerant than general war could have made it.

Early in the seventh century Mohammedanism began to be a power in the east, and destined to overwhelm the Armenians as a nation and bring about the dispersion which continues to this day. From this time the history of the country is the story of alien sovereigns, while the passing of the sceptre from the hands of native princes is almost imperceptible in the pages of history. Yet we exist as a people, and, amid the revolutions of the eastern world, we firmly retain our national characteristics and are ever true to Christianity. The pomp, glory and wealth of ages gone, the sceptre passed to the conqueror's grasp, there is left but the cherished cross of martyrdom, the emblem of national unity and hope of eternal reward.

The first invasion of the Mohammedans occurred in 638, in the province of Daron. The Armenians could ill afford, in their weakened condition, to make a stand against these fierce warriors. So they made a compromise with the Saracens, by the terms of which they were to enjoy the Christian religion unmolested. The Greek co-religionists of the Armenians took up arms against them and threatened extermination as the penalty for their affiliation with the Mohammedans on any terms. War was only averted by the most solemn pledges of fidelity to the Greeks. A common religion removed the prejudices and jealousies of centuries first engendered by the Armenians co-operating with Xerxes in his invasion of Greece (859 A. D.), and Ashod of the Pagratid dynasty became king by consent of Caliph and the Emperor of Constantinople, and his decendents ruled until 1070 A. D., when control of the territory passed to Constantinople.

A small kingdom remained in the Taurus mountains until 1375, when Leon VI., last of the Armenian kings, was captured and banished. After six years in Egypt, he traveled through Europe until the time of his death in Paris, 1393.* He had co-operated with the Crusaders and with the king of Cyprus, and was the last bulwark of armed Christianity in the east. His kingdom was known

---

* The author, when in Paris, visited his tomb. What thoughts fill the mind, what feelings move the heart of an Armenian youth as he stands in a strange land by the grave of the last of the noble kings of his countrymen, who had dared to draw his sword in defence of his people and their religion. It is said that his body, clad in robes of white, with a golden sceptre placed within his hand and an opal crown upon his head, was carried to the tomb in regal pomp. Thus sadly doth the unseemly show of death's procession mock at life's stern realities.

as Lesser Armenia. Since it fell the Armenians have been a people without a country, but everywhere upholding the cross with singular fidelity.

About 2,500,000 of our people are still in the Ottoman Empire. An equal number may be found in other parts of the world—India, Persia, Russia and European countries.

Social purity of a high order obtains with us. We have no illegitimate births, no divorce court, customs and ancient law being against it. Such matters are in the jurisdiction of the Church and are regulated in the interests of the family. Jealousy may be said to be a national curse, but a universal religion binds the nation in a common tie.

The frequent reference by Amenian and Greek writers to their respective people as a nation, is not understood by most Americans without some account of the Mohammedan system of administering the internal affairs of the Sultan's realm.

By the policy of the Porte, the Armenians, Greeks, Roman Catholics, Protestants and Jews are merely subject nations, paying tribute to the ruling Moslem element.

Armenians are responsible to their religious leaders, who are represented by the patriarch at the sublime Porte. Only the "faithful" or Moslems are allowed in the army, Armenians gaining exemptment by the paying of a tax. The result of this plan is altogether favorable to the Armenians, and they have doubled in number during the past fifty years; while the Mohammedan population has remained stationary owing to the large sacrifice of young men engaged in military service. The sanitary arrangement of camps is usually bad, disease claiming more victims than battlefields. There is thus always a surplus of females. Moreover, while Mohammedan women are kind and affectionate mothers, their lack of education results in a heavy death rate among children.

The mutual jealousies of Christians of various creeds led to great abuse of the powers vested in their representatives, who had influence enough to cause the arrest and banishment of apostates who were siding with Protestant missionaries.

Some Americans, unintentionally perhaps, confuse the Armenians with the Turks, just as some of our people presume the Americans to be the civilized sons of once uncivilized North Armerican Indians. Nothing is more offensive to an Armenian than to be called a Turk. It is no more right to call an Armenian a Turk than to call him an Italian. Though they may live in the same country, yet there is an essential difference between the Armenians and the Turks in race, nationality, religion, language, manners and customs, in truth almost in every respect.

Ethnologists treat of Aryans and Turanians among the primative human families, as to either their complexion or intelligence. Armenians, known as the "Anglo-Saxons of the East," with the progressive nations of the western civilization, belong to the Aryan, while the Turks, with a mighty host of Asiatics, belong to the Turanian race.

There is no social intercourse, nor is there any intermarriage between these two nationalities.

As a nation, we have been separate and distinct from the Turanian element throughout all ages. Our lost nationality is not dead.

The Turks originated from numerous nomadic tribes of Central Asia, but from the fact that they have no authentic history, we can not precisely determine from what tribes they have descended. In religion the Armenians are Christian, and have been Christians ever since there was Christianity, while the Turks are Mohammedan, and there are not to-day in the entire country a dozen Turkish Christians, nor are there one-half dozen Armenian Mohammedans. In language, Armenian is as much differentiated from Turkish as English from Chinese. So let us clearly bear in mind that they are two distinct nationalities, separate in race, religion, language, aspect, manners and character.

Armenians are the only brilliant star twinkling in the dark horizon of the Orient. No matter under-what skies or flags I wander, I am ever proud of my nationality. We, the Armenians, from the remotest antiquity have been the most religious and liberty-loving people on the face of the earth. The characteristics of our people are considered far superior to those of the nations about us. In this, almost all modern and ancient historians, travellers and missionaries are unanimous. Let me quote but two testimonials concerning our people. The famous author, Emile De Laveleye says, in "The Balkan Peninsula":

"The Armenians are intelligent, laborious, economical and excellent business men. They occupy official appointments in the administration of the Ottoman Empire, and in Constantinople they are the chief promoters of economical activity. Their civilization is among the oldest in Asia. Their annals date from the earliest historic times."

The late Rev. H. G. O. Dwight, D. D., one of the pioneer missionaries of the American Board among our people, reflects observations of many years in these words: "They (Armenians) have shown themselves to be superior to any other race in commercial tact and in mechanical skill. The principal merchants are Armenians, and nearly all the great bankers of the government; and, whatever arts there are that require peculiar ingenuity and skill, they are almost sure to be in the hands of the Armenians. . . . In one word, they are the Anglo-Saxons of the East."

I cannot close this chapter on the fortunes of my people without an appeal to that great Cosmopolitan nation, the secret of whose marvelous unity is freedom and intelligence, to aid in the enlightenment, encouragement and consequent liberation of a people, kindred though remote, who, through the thick fogs of ignorance and gloom of oppression, have kept intact the love of liberty, the very font of manhood, together with those qualities that make good citizenship, strength and sobriety.

ARMENIAN LITERATURE.

"The Armenian literature is rich and continuous, uninterrupted through all the middle ages. It has furnished the philosophers, historians, theologians and poets."—*Prof. Emile De Laveleye.*

FOLK-LORE, the mother of literature, with its legends and simple rural songs, forms the fountain head of every nation's purest thought and noblest sentiment. A country's scenery, its lofty mountains, green hills and fertile valleys exerts an influence upon the physical conditions and intellectual standards of a people that cannot be overestimated. Switzerland, with its grand, uplifting heights, is famed for the inborn love of liberty cherished by its people. Every Anglo-Saxon knows the songs of Robert Burns, inspired among the highlands of Scotland. Each lad and lassie is thrilled by the soft, sweet tones of his æolian harp. Armenia has her bards, whose songs are enriched by the natural scenery which first echoed their refrain. The native poet's passion for birds and flowers inspires his every line, while the varied perfumes of the fields breathes from many a stanza.

Long, long ere letters were invented, the enraptured

heart of the poet broke forth in song, the rythem so complete that not a word could be changed without destroying the sense. Was it not so with blind Homer? Armenia's heritage of song is her richest treasure, bequeathed by misty figures in the pre-historic past. So ancient are her melodies that they seem the breath of her body and the light of her soul.

Her mountains, hills and valleys, her birds and flowers, her kings and battles, even the broken heart-strings of her stricken mothers, are unutterably woven into the strain of poesy. Native poetry finds here its strong incentive. Grim, slothful winter lingers long, holding gentle spring in his icy grasp. She rises suddenly in her youthful strength, and snowflakes change to flowers with a suddenness that surprises the stranger. The quick transition, this annual resurrection, is the theme of many a bard. Spring poetry is addressed to the stork, as harbinger of the season, who, when he comes to stay, brings summer with him.

The ancients dedicated spring to the goddess Amahid. All the people joined in the feast of *Varthavar*, rose blossoms. Since Christian times, this has been supplanted by the three days' festival of the Transfiguration. The former ancient custom, the feast of Rose Blossoms, indicates the love of the beautiful, which leads to the true, and can have its origin only in the good. There is a religious halo about the very name of flowers. The Fountain's Blood is a floral wonder. Was it the blood of righteous Abel that sprang from the ground as this crimson flower on a leafless stalk, calling to God in its blood-red simplicity for vengeance on the murderer? All these beauties of the field and glen have called forth exquisite gems of thought, which are treasured to this day.

There is a sad Armenian elegy on Adam's expulsion from Paradise, in theme not unlike portions of Milton's 'Paradise

NATURE'S SONG.

Lost.' But our poets have seldom wandered into the realm of fancy—their themes are of the heart, varying with the fortunes of the people as a nation, from a tone of joyful victory to that of subdued melancholy, which, however, never descends to despair, whatever the adversity.

The whole literary fabric is imbued with a religious

faith in the final justice of God, which finds no parallel, except in the literature of the Hebrew race. A literal translation of the following stanza does not destroy the poetic thought and religious hope which saves from despair a wounded mother grieving for her child. Unfortunately, translation injures the effect of the original:

> "I gaze and weep, mother of my boy,
>   I say alas and woe is me!
> What will become of wretched me
>   I have seen my golden son dead!
> They seized that fragrant rose
>   Of my breast, and my soul fainted away;
> They let that beautiful golden dove
>   Fly away, and my heart was wounded.
> The falcon Death seized
>   My dear and sweet-voiced turtle dove and wounded me.
> They took my sweet-toned little lark
>   And flew away through the skies!
> Before my eyes they sent the hail
>   On my flowering green promegranate,
> My rosy apple on the tree,
>   Which gives fragrance among the leaves.
> They shook my flourishing beautiful almond tree
>   And left me without fruit;
> Beating it they threw it on the ground
>   And trod it under foot into the earth of the grave.
> What, what will become of wretched me!
>   Many sorrows surrounded me.
> O, my God, receive the soul of my little one
>   And place him at rest in Thy bright heaven."

The simple pathos and exquisite conception of bird and flower analogies by the rural bards are touchingly illustrated in the above selection. The birds of Armenia, like the flowers, are countless in number and variety. Her poets seldom write without embellishing their lines with reference to some of their feathered or fragrant friends of the field. The partridge is a special favorite, as the following stanzas would indicate :

> "Thy nest is enamelled with flowers,
>   With vasilico, narcissus, and water-lily;
> Thy place is full of dew,
>   Thou delightest in the fragrant odor.
> Ah! pretty, pretty,
>   Ah! dear little partridge!
>
> When the little partridge descends from the tree,
>   And with his sweet voice chirps,
> He cheers all the world,
>   He draws the heart from the sea of blood.
> Ah! pretty, pretty,
>   Ah! dear little partridge!
>
> All the birds call thee blessed,
>   They come with thee in flocks,
> They come around thee chirping;
>   In truth there is not one like thee.
> Ah! pretty, pretty,
>   Ah! beautiful little partridge!

The crane is the harbinger of summer as the stork is of spring, and has received his share of poetic tribute.

To the Armenian, under foreign skies, the flight of the crane is alway suggestive of home. His thoughts will be such as to recall the poets of his Oriental fatherland. "Crane, whence comest thou? Hast thou no news of our country?"

Thanks to the modern scientific research, news flies faster than the crane, and the Armenian in America is abreast with the times on the Armenian question and has the news before the Armenian residents on the foot-hills of Ararat can possibly get it.

The tender regard of Armenians for the birds of the air has its origin in the ancient superstition of transmigration. Among the ignorant, it is still believed that the spirits of the departed in the form of birds visit the scenes of their

A SCENE IN ARMENIA.

youth. For this reason the denizens of the air are seldom disturbed by the Armenian peasants. Many of the most touching poetical illusions in regard to them, are born of the idea that they are custodians of the the spirits of departed friends.

The limpid, laughing waters of Armenia's swift descending streams as they babble through rocky channels, or bound from shelving precipice in a musical cascade, have shared the laureat's fancy with the star reflecting blue of the crystal lakes. A hearty expression of the poetic charms of a mountain torrent, watering fields and gardens in the lower valley, is the following :

>"Down from yon distant mountain
>　The water flows through the village, Ha!
>A dark boy comes forth,
>　And washes his hands and face,
>Washing, yes washing,
>　And turning to the water, asked, Ha!
>Water, from what mountain dost thou come?
>　O my cool and sweet water! Ha!
>I come from that mountain,
>　Where the old and new snow lie one on the other.
>
>"Water, to what garden dost thou go ?
>　O my cool and sweet water! Ha!
>I go into that garden
>　Where there is the sweet song of the nightingale! Ha!
>Water, into what fountain dost thou go?
>　O my cool and sweet little water!
>I go to that fountain
>　Where thy love comes and drinks.
>I go to meet her and kiss her lips,
>　And satiate myself with her love."

To dramatic poetry the Armenian singer frequently turns. Many examples of this branch of the art are connected with the famous Lake Van, around which countless traditions are woven. An excellent example of this class of poetry is given below :

"We sailed in the ship from Aghthamar.
We directed our ship towards Avan;
When we arrived before Vosdan
We saw the dark sun of the dark day.

Dull clouds covered the sky,
Obscuring at once stars and moon;
The winds blew fiercely,
And took from my eyes land and home.

Thundered the heaven, thundered the earth,
The waters of the blue sea arose;
On every side the heavens shot forth fire;
Black terror invaded my heart.

There is the sky, but the earth is not seen,
There is the earth, but the sun is not seen·
The waves come like mountains
And open before me a deep abyss.

O see, if thou lovest thy God,
Have pity on me, forlorn and wretched;
Take not from me my sweet sun,
And betray me not to flinty-hearted Death.

Pity, O sea, O terrible sea!
Give me not up to the cold winds:
My tears implore thee
And the thousand sorrows of my heart . . .

The savage sea has no pity!
It hears not the plaintive voice of my broken heart;
The blood freezes in my veins,
Black night descends upon my eyes . . .

Go tell to my mother
To sit and weep for her darkened son;
That John was the prey of the sea,
The sun of the young man is set!

Summer! The short, sweet, seductive summer of Armenia does not last long enough to produce ennui.

THE PASSING OF SUMMER.

This brief, bright pageantry of blooming, fragrant flowers and ripening fruit, comes quickly, does its work in haste, and departs while a chill, gloomy winter succeeds, suppressing autumn before it fairly has a chance to exist.

How much the utter seclusion of Armenian domiciles, apart from the centers of population, has had to do in developing, through the long winter for meditation, the poetic instinct, we can well surmise. These patriarchal abodes are snow-bound from October until May, and from such retreats chiefly have come the ancient and modern literature of Armenia.

There is great paucity of Armenian written literature prior to the Christian era. However, we have proof that the national enthusiasm for knowledge is not of modern inspiration. A people so proud will not willingly let their deeds of valor on hard fought fields die unrecorded. The names of heroes and sages were household words at every family altar and fireside.

Cherished names and historical events garnered in national songs and stories, were handed from generation to generation as sacred traditions for centuries, until the art of writing became common.

Modern archæologists have discovered and read ancient cuneiform records, which bear a remarkable analogy to the traditionary lore. Assyrian, Greek and Hebrew records help to fill in the missing links in an almost unbroken chain, so that Armenian tradition may be said to more nearly approach historical literature in value than that of any other nation of the earth. The unwritten history of the masses is confirmed in most essential points, at least by the modern reading of records of the few who were able to record the facts of history on the face of the rocks among the everlasting hills. Time has dealt kindly with those precious records, and the curious student may find full account of their discovery in the annals of archæology.

Like the tombs of Egypt, the cradle of the human race is slowly but surely giving up the secrets of thousands of years. The earliest and most valued of our historical sources is the work of Agathangaegos, who flourished in the third century of our era. He was the private secretary of King Tiridates of Armenia.

The rarest manuscripts I have seen are found in the alcoves of Armenian monastic libraries. About two thousand of them are preserved at Etchmiazin, one thousand two hundred in the convent of St. Lazaro at Venice; the Royal Library at Paris, through the emissaries of Louis XIV., contains about two hundred of them; Bodleian Library and British Museum contain but a few manuscripts.

Many of these manuscripts are the work of inferior or little-known writers, but all of them have a high value because of their great age and the painstaking care with which the laborious work of copying was done.

In the fifth century, A. D., Moses of Chorene, by his historical writings, became the Herodotus of the Armenian people. He treasured in his works the traditional history of his time, some parts of which continued to be handed down orally as of yore, the fidelity and accuracy with

ARMENIAN LITERATURE. 99

which the people transmitted them being much to their credit.

In the same century, a period of unusual intellectual activity, St. Mesrob, an illustrious prelate of an Armenian monastery, modified the alphabet to its present form, composed of thirty-eight letters. He is sometimes called its inventor, which gives him more honor than is his due. Prior to his introduction of the Armenian letters, the Greek alphabet was in use by our nation. The Armenian is an inflected language, with four conjugations and twelve declensions. It belongs to the Aryan branch of Indo-Germanic family of languages. In syntactical structure, the classical Armenian bears a close resemblance to the ancient Greek. It has no grammatical gender or dual form.

Espousing Christianity early in our race, we experienced with that change a great revival of literary and intellectual activity, the first fruits of which were numerous translations of the sacred stories from Syriac and Greek. Armenian students were seen at all the educational centers of Europe, Alexandria and Byzantium. To their translations are due the preservation in Armenia of many valuable writings, extinct in the original and all other tongues.

The Old Testament was translated by Sahak the Patriarch, from the Septuagint version. There are conflicting opinions concerning the final accomplishment of what is known as the "Queen of Versions." Some parts are evidently from the Syriac and some from the Greek, but the greater part is from Septuagint. The sixth century may well be called the dormant era of Armenian literature. All intercourse with Greek centers of learning being cut off by the Persians, the pursuit of literature declined in its avidity.

During the seventh century several valuable historical and theological works were written. In the eighth century John of Osdin and Stephanus of Siunia were leading writers, while in the ninth, John the Catholicos, Thomas Ardzruni, and several others enriched the literature of the country.

The tenth was equally productive of leaders of thought through the medium of the pen. In the eleventh, Aristakes of Lastiverd, the national historian, flourished with numerous contemporaries; among them Matthew Yeretz, the biographer of Chrysostom. The twelfth and thirteenth centuries, in which Syriac influence predominated, was a second period of great literary activity. Later the Armenians of the west gave their literature such names as Rivola (1633), Villote, La Croze, Osgan and others, who were eclipsed by St. Martin. In Russia and France, Armenians ranked among the best writers; Speigle, Justi, Neumann and Pertermann in Germany have made enviable reputations.

In the present century the work of Armenian Romish monks of the convent St. Lazaro, Venice, may well rank first. This convent is the cradle of ancient and modern Armenian literature. Many translations from European languages have been issued from this place along with valuable books of reference, dictionaries, and works of similar nature. The convent is particularly interesting to modern students and tourists, because it was there that Byron sojourned for a time, deeply interesting himself in Armenian literature and its expounders, the learned monks. This remarkable establishment has been greatly distinguished for its eminent services in the cause of morality and learning. In 1810, when a general order for the suppression of all monastic institutions in Venice was issued, St. Lazaro alone was exempted from its sweeping effects. Another proof of the high estimation in which the monastery stands, is shown by the fact that the Pope made it his usual custom to confer upon each new abbot of St. Lazaro the title and dignity of Archbishop, although the prelate has neither province nor subordinate clergy under him.

American missionaries have furnished scientific text books and are increasing the number from time to time. An Armenian who can afford them may have as good a practical library in his native language as the artizan or merchant could desire. From these facts some interesting conclusions can be drawn.

Through four-fifths of the Christian era, Armenian literature has enjoyed a more perfect continuity than that of any other Christian nation.

When Europe was passing through the dark ages, the Christian Armenians of the Orient were enjoying a season of unparalleled intellectual activity, creating for mankind a literature of no little value, and the day may yet come when her purest songs and highest thought may be ranked among those classics which are not the possession of any tongue or people, but have in them so much of man's heart and life that they belong to man as the legacy of the race.

THE ARMENIAN CHURCH.

" The Armenians may justly claim to be the oldest Christian nation in the world."—*H. B. Tristram, D. D., LL. D., F. R. S., Canon of Durham, England.*

BEFORE entering into a description of the Armenian church, let us cast a glance at the various stages of the primitive religious life of the people. From the earliest times man has recognized and obeyed the religious instinct. Conscience and reason, no matter how rudimentary, combine to make him bow before some power outside himself, in whose hands he is, and to whom he owes some sort of homage. The veriest savage acknowledges with mingled fear and gratitude his dependence upon the Great Provider, Ordainer and Judge, if only in his reverence for the Son. As this religious impulse develops, the idea of propitiation forms more and more the predominant element in it, probably from the growing sense of helplessness and fate consequent upon the accumulation of experience.

Once this idea of propitiation has firmly seized upon the primitive mind, the next step is, for the sake of greater efficiency, to dedicate all this work to one man—judged pleasing to the gods.

This is the idea of the priest—simple at first and pure. Often this priest was merely the head of the family, who, as the revered, obeyed and responsible representative thereof, stood therefore before the gods to recommend, to intercede, and conversely to bless and to curse. Such was the earliest form of Oriental priesthood.

According to the testimony of the Scriptures, after the resting of the ark "upon the mountains of Ararat," Noah offered burnt offerings upon the altar. Since these mountains are in our central province, Armenia may be said to be the earliest home of divine worship, and from here patriarchial monotheism was transmitted to Noah's descendants.

In the centuries following, we frequently meet with analagous cases of Abraham and of kindred patriarchs as worshipers of one true God. In the patriarchal observance of religion, the father was the high priest of the family, officiating daily at the rude family altar. He enjoyed the sacred religious reverence which is the divine right of the pious head of a family. We may well pray for restoration of this ancient and mutual sense of religious duty and respect in many a modern home.

The Old Testament is not a universal history. It is the history of the Hebrew nation. It does not, therefore, mention all nations who were possessed of the same form of worship. But we have our traditions, which are sufficient proof to sustain us in our belief that pure monotheism was the pre-historic religion of the Armenians, as it was the primitive religion of all other Aryans. We cannot, however, positively determine the duration of that pure religion in Armenia. By degrees, through the influence of idolatrous neighbors, she embraced polytheism of Assyro-Babylonian type. Our cuneiform inscriptions inform us in particular of the names of deities and the regulations for daily sacrifice.

With the supremacy of the Medo-Persian empire, there arose in Western Asia the dualistic religion of Zoroaster, teaching that there are two supernatural beings—Ormazd,* the creator and preserver of all things good, and Ahriman, the source of all evil and mischief. These rival gods, having in command good and evil spirits, were in perpetual strife. The fire, which was the personification of Ormazd's son, became the supreme object of worship.

This was the religion of the Armenians from the last decade of the seventh century B. C. to the advent and introduction of Christianity, in whose cause our people struggled in many bloody battles against the established Zoroasterian system.

The Armenian church is of vital interest to Armenians, because it has served a double mission. Not only is it an organization exerting a religious influence on the people, but since the subjection of the country to the Turkish government, the church has also served as a conservator of the national spirit and unity.

Patriotism and common religion are two important uniting forces of a nation, and of the two, religion is far

---

* Ormazd of the Persians is the same as Armazt of the Armenians and Jupiter of the Greeks.

more potent in its preserving power. Although under the Turkish yoke, the Armenians still preserve their national peculiarities; they are independent in spirit if not in fact. But this church should also be of interest to every Christian of every country, because of its associations with early Christianity. It should be a delight to trace down the centuries and fortunes and misfortunes of a church founded by the first disciples of our Saviour.

Cast a glance at the condition of the eastern world in the time of Christ's Advent! When Zoroastrianism was multiplying its gods, and at the same time multiplying vice and immorality, when the ancient Babylonians were in eager endeavor to keep their old, dying Sabaism alive, when many branches of heathenism were contemplating the manufacture of some new and better gods, when even the sacred religion of Judaism had fallen into ritualistic literalism; in a word, when the dark and threatening clouds of meaningless strife and hopeless controversy had seized the oriental sky, and the people were blundering in the darkness of superstition and ignorance, then rose the Son of Righteousness to illumine the whole world, bearing in its radiance the burden of that angelic benediction, "Peace on earth, good will toward men."

It was during the reign of our King Abgarus of Edessa that Bartholomew, one of the twelve, and Thaddeus, one of the seventy, went about preaching the gospel in Armenia. As a result of their faithful labors and the power of the new Gospel they proclaimed, the king and the royal family were converted and baptized in the river Euphrates, and following their example, the whole nation turned from their idolatry to the true God.

Notwithstanding this resistless wave of Christain power and good, the conversion proved transient, and a short time after the death of Abgarus the nation relapsed into its false religion. It was reserved for St. Gregory, a prince of the reigning family of Arsacidae, a man "mighty to the Lord," to turn the erring people back to Christian faith and worship. This learned man had been sent by Tiridates to the Greek bishops of Cæsarea for ordination, and under the influence of his preaching, the haughty king Tiridates (Durtad) embraced Christianity, and as a result, each man became iconoclast, and worshiped again a spirit in spirit and in truth (301 A. D.)*

Tiridates bestowed on his people the imperishable honor of being the first nation to have a Christian ruler. The baptism of this Armenian king into the Christian church antedates that of Constantine thirty-seven years. Commonly the latter is referred to as the first Christian emperor, through paucity of information on Armenian history in the libraries of Europe and America.

With Christianity came an elevation of the national mind, and the century following formed the golden age of Armenian literature. Schools were established in every

---

*The converting the king by St. Gregory is most remarkable in the light of the fact that Gregory's father had assassinated the father of the king, who was the assassin's cousin.

part of the country, and as a crowning triumph the Bible was translated into the Armenian language. Our bishops sat in all the early councils of the one common Christian church, catholic in spirit, liberal in doctrine and government.

About 450 A. D., various causes presented Armenia's representation in the fourth Ecumenical Council of Chalcedon, at which Eutyches was condemned on the doctrine relating to the person of Christ. The Armenian church reserved their decision, and was assumed to endorse his heresy, which was untrue. In 491 this doctrine in full Synod was formally annulled by our patriarch, which act resulted in separation from the Greek and Roman churches. It was not a question of dogma, but of jurisdiction, that caused it to reject the council. Documentary evidence is not wanting to show that the Armenian church was essentially orthodox at that time and has ever been so. European and American historians have drawn on bigoted Latin and Greek sources for the information. On the contrary, so long as the Armenian church stands aloft from the endorsement of the Council of Chalcedon, her autocracy is secure. To concur would be to court absorption into the Greek and Roman hierarchies.

When we consider with what the Armenian church has had to contend during the past eighteen centuries, our sympathies cannot fail to be awakened and our admiration kindled. The time came when the Persian conquerors offered annihilation by the sword or religious submission to forsaken heathenism. A most critical moment; they must wade through a carnage of death to religious freedom, or desert the pure religion of their fathers! Christian homes or Christian graves was the unanimous sentiment that echoed from the Armenian ranks. Men, women, children, all stood on the battle ground in defence of their faith. One universal resolution prevailed, "From this belief no one can move us, neither angels nor men, neither fire nor sword, nor water, nor any other horrid tortures." What a pathetic scene! In that vast throng of clergy and laity, Prince Vartan Mamigonian, the valiant commander-in-chief of the Christian host, lifted his eloquent voice in a thrilling oration: "I entreat you, my brave companions," said he, "fear not the number of the heathen, withdraw not your necks from the terrific sword of a mortal man! That the Lord may give the victory into our hands, that we may annihilate their power and lift on high the standard of truth."

In the morning, with clash of arms the army of the Persians was advancing. No time could be lost, the decisive battle was soon on! It was after partaking of the holy communion that the Armenians marched on with brave hearts and with these words on their lips, "May our death be like the death of the just, and may the shedding of our blood resemble the blood-shedding of the prophets! May God look in mercy on our voluntary self-offering, and may He not deliver the Church into the hands of the heathen." The battle raged furiously. Never fought men with greater

THE ARMENIAN CHURCH. 109

heroism, though fewer in number, and though their noble commander was first among the slain, the courage of the determined heroes of the Cross increased until they shook the Persian throne to its foundation, and the Persian monarch, retreating in confusion, besought compromise, granting religious liberty. This was the last of many religious battles in which the Armenians contended with opposing Zoroastrianism, and they dealt her here such a blow that she never again lifted her hand to strike. Persecuted as she has been by the relentless Saracen, and by the still more murderous Mongol and Tartar, she has always held her ground patiently, heroically, and songs of hallelujah she has sung above all the strife and conflict. Not with inward controversies, but with the red blood of martyrdom have Armenians maintained their religion throughout all ages. Tangible good resulted from the long centuries of persecution. It strengthened the faithful. An iron-clad Christian character resulted, successfully resisting the sensual allurements of Islamism for generations. Western Christians may frequently be seen to embrace Mohammedanism for military or social standing, but the Armenian almost never!

For many centuries the Church suffered the meddlesome interference of the Pope at Rome, who tried to place it in subordination to the papal power. Many apostacised to Rome (notably since the Council of Florence, 1439 A. D.), perhaps in the hope of the better protection of a stronger and more dominant organization; undoubtedly the superior schools of the Jesuits also attracted a large number from the National Church. Nor is this all; owing to the continued opposition and interference of the Greek Church, much of its superstition has crept in and has exerted a pernicious influence on the national religion, robbing it of its pristine purity and simplicity. In the twelfth century Merses Lambronasses, a celebrated Armenian orator, in a masterly speech, advocated the union of the two churches. The laity and clergy, however, unanimously rejected the idea, suspecting that it threatened their independence. Moreover, the doctrines and usages of the two churches differ widely in many particulars. While the Armenian Church claims to be orthodox, she does not claim to be the only orthodox church, and does not deny communion to members of Greek and Roman churches. The Armenian Church is liberal, while the Greek is exclusive in the extreme.

Whether owing his allegiance to Rome or to the orthodox Greek, a convert to the evangelical missions, or yet within the fold of the native church, the Armenian Christian still esteems Etchmiadzin the most sacred shrine of national adoration. The monastery of Etchmiadzin, most ancient of monastic foundations, has been the patriarchial throne of Armenia throughout all Christian ages. Here is the first St. Gregory's church, traditionally founded on a spot where Christ descended, as its name implies, "Etch" meaning descent, and "miadzin" only-begotten. It is at the foot of Mount Ararat, cruciform, with transcepts so short that it seems square. It is elaborately decorated with ornaments usual to Armenian places of worship.

Of all the officers of the church, the Catholicos ranks highest, the Catholicos at at Etchmiadzin being supreme.*

MGR. KHRIMIAN, CATHOLICOS OF ALL ARMENIANS.

* The author, when in Constantinople, had the pleasure of an extended interview with the ex-patriarch, Mgr. Khrimian, who has been recently exalted to the office of Catholicos at Etchmiadzin. He was cordially received and enjoyed the paternal advice and blessing of this highest dignitary of the Armenian church and people. When about to depart, the venerable man presented his young congenere with several original autograph volumes, which are held as priceless additions to his library.

This personage is executively of somewhat papal authority. However, no dogma of infallibility deifies him. After being elected by all the archbishops, he must be confirmed by the Czar of Russia, who guarantees him protection and enforces his decrees.

There are also other Catholicos at Sis, in the ancient province of Cicilia, and at Akhtamar, upon an island of Lake Van, and two Patriarchs, one at Constantinople and the other at Jerusalem. The function of the Patriarch is more of a political nature, representing the Armenian nation and church to the authorities. Ecclesiastically he holds the rank of a Bishop. Next in order are the archbishops and bishops, who are elected to their office by the entire nation and ordained by the Catholicos. Formerly it was the custom to ordain these officers at Cæsarea or Sis, but in the patriarchate of Nerses the Great, who lived 363 A. D., this custom was discarded by the sentiment of the laity and the present practice inaugurated.

After ordination, the bishop confines himself in a room of the church, fasting and praying for about two weeks, when he is prepared to enter upon his duties. During this time he studies the ritual and forms of the church, and at its conclusion is possessed of the power of absolution. The bishops are much more highly educated than the priests, being elected from an order known as *Vartabets*, or doctors of theology. Indeed, the *Vartabets* represent the highest culture of the nation, and to them it is indebted for most of its literature. The priest is chosen by the people from

THE ARMENIAN CHURCH.   113

among themselves, and is supposed to possess a good education and knowledge of the Bible. He is, as a rule, a venerable man with a long beard.

Celibacy is not compulsory, but a priest can not rise

AN ARMENIAN BISHOP.

higher than his order while his wife is living. He performs the marriage ceremony, administers baptism, officiates at funerals and takes charge of the morning and evening services of the church. He receives no salary, but depends on contributions for his support. It can easily be imagined why we have no wealthy priests. The Armenian monks are of the order of St. Basil.

As has been indicated before, the Armenian Church is Apostolic, orthodox in its form, Episcopal and liberal in its nature. In theology it is Augustinian, adopting the Apostolic, the Nicene and the Athanasian creeds. It has more affinity now to the Church of England than to any other.

It embraces the doctrine of the Trinity, and believes in the incarnated divinity of Christ, separated but blended in perfect harmony in an unapproachable life. It declares that the holy spirit is an essence emanating from God, and that it is the source of union between God and man. It believes in the adoration and mediation of saints, but not in the purgatorial penance, though prayer and entreaties are offered for the pardon of departed souls. Contrary to the Greek and Roman churches, it places the Bible in the hands of all the people, believing in the potency of the inspired word for the conviction and salvation of souls.

Every morning at sunrise and every evening at sunset the people assemble in the churches and regular services are held. The scriptures are chanted or read. The sermon is usually preached and the ceremonies performed in the ancient Armenian tongue. This part of the service is not given the prominence it receives in this country, and it is not uncommon for the people to go home before or even during the preaching, because of the lengthy liturgy. The

THE ARMENIAN CHURCH. 115

sign of the cross is used at all services. The adoration of the pictures of saints and the cross is believed to be of special efficacy. The church liturgy, though ancient and extensive, is yet most beautiful in style and in religious sentiment.

There are seven sacraments—baptism, confirmation, the eucharist, penance, ordination, marriage and extreme unction. The Armenian Church practices a triple immersion of infants, and teaches that by it original sin is washed away, while actual sin requires auricular confession and penance. Confirmation is administered immediately after baptism, the child being anointed with holy oil. The doctrine of Transubstantiation is regarded as extremely important, unleavened bread being used in the sacrament and dipped in undiluted wine.

Penance consists in fasting, which occurs every Wednesday and Friday, and also in abstaining from eggs and meat of all kinds. Confession to the priesthood constitutes a necessary preparation for participation in the sacrament of the Lord's Supper.

There are also many sacred holidays, among which is Christmas, celebrated on the eighteenth of January; Nativity and Epiphany on the sixth. Extreme unction is administered only to the ecclesiastics.

Like the children of erring Israel, the Armenians have wandered often and far from the primitive faith, and yet we can but admire the heroism with which they have contended for their religion and church? With the introduction of Christianity we can bid a final adieu to the pagan influence in the social and religious life of the Armenians, for having given up their idols and torn down temples of Bael, they took up the cross never to lay it down. That church has for its corner-stone Christ Jesus, and rests on the firm foundation of the inspired revelation. But to the truth has been added much superstition, and the religion once so full of spirit and devotion, has lapsed into mere formalism, which is fatal to every Christian grace and fruit. Armenia still upholds her torch, but it emits no gracious light; while yet the knee is bent to the one true God, the spirit kneels not to its King. The voice of the disciples here heard so long ago inspires no more, and the fire kindled in the souls of men has almost sunk to ashes. How sad to think that she who gave so much is poor to-day in what so freely she bestowed! and yet it need not be so.

While Christian nations are seeking to save the lost in darker lands, let them not forget their obligation to Armenia; from her freely they have received, and now, in her dire necessity, should they not freely give? The occidental Christendom, which to-day enjoys the peace, love and cordial fellowship of Christianity—so cheap, so easy, so honorable; do they not owe something to our Oriental pioneer, who "fought to win the prize, and sailed through bloody seas?" And not only is it an obligation but a privilege to evangelize a land, the scene of the Apostles' first efforts.

Armenia's earnest appeal should not fall lightly on the

Christian world. She does not ask for much, but she pleads for the listening ear and the helping hand of Christendom. Obviously the church needs reform in many particulars, and none are so aware of this as the earnest native Christian preachers.

In Armenia the Bible is and has been in the hands of the people, and their customs and life are permeated with its leavening principles. Thus the obstacle with which foreign missionaries usually have had to contend are not found here. Armenia is destined to great awakening. Christian missions have flourished and increased here as in no other land. Let hands be clasped across the wide ocean that separates us, and let Christendom harken once more to the cry that comes in the night, "Come over and help us."

THE EVANGELICAL CHURCH.

"Come over and help us."—*Macedonia Cry*.

THE labor of evangelization among the Armenians has been in its nature fundamentally different from that of most mission countries.

No heathen idolatry was here with which to contend. No wooden gods and massive temples built of ignorant superstition were to be torn down before Christianity could be introduced and a true God preached. The people already worshiped the God of the Christian; the spiritual kingdom needed not a revolution so much as a reformation, and it is with complacency that Armenia can point to one of her own sons as the instigator and founder of the reformatory movement. We refer to a native priest living near Constantinople, who in the year 1760 put forth a manuscript copy of a book whose every page breathed the spirit of dissatisfaction with the existing state of religious life. Besides speaking in commendatory terms of the great reformer, Martin Luther, it pointed out many errors into which the Church had gradually fallen, and urged that a reform of some sort was eminently necessary. This, though for some reason never printed, wielded a salutary influence in the minds of the people, especially among the higher clergy, many of whom were inspired by it to action more or less effective.

One of the indications that would point to the spiritual lethargy of the times was the extreme rarity of Bibles; and here we take occasion to say that no true and active Christian life is possible without some communion with that stimulator of the soul's higher existence, the Word of God. It was a most healthful sign when an urgent want began to be expressed for more copies of the sacred book, and it was also a very encouraging expression of the pulse of Christendom when the British and Russian Bible societies, at about the same time, proffered their help in the field white unto harvest. As an outcome of the self-sacrificing interest of these two organizations, in the year 1823 about 20,000 copies of the Scriptures were translated into the language. The Armenian people will ever gratefully remember this timely service. It was soon perceived, however, that much more good would be accomplished were the translations made in modern Armenian rather than in the ancient tongue. The latter the common people were not able to read, and most of the copies published of necessity fell into the hands of priests and monks. The former, the modern Armenian, is understood by educated and uneducated alike, and the Bible societies referred to did a very wise thing in putting forth another version adapted to the needs of clergymen and laborers, poor and rich alike.

The pioneer work in any mission country is placing in the hands of its people the Word in their vernacular. It is the foundation for the future edifice, the sowing for the future harvest, and the distribution of the Scriptures at this time was not without its significant fruit in later years, for it has not only produced a better morality, not merely the means of spiritual life, but it has also given impetus to mental activity.

We now come to that which is most interesting to those who probably comprise the majority of the readers of this book—the work of the American Board of Foreign Missions. Missionary Parsons met at Jerusalem in 1821, several Armenians, who, according to a custom still in vogue, were on a pilgrimage thither. Becoming interested in them, he proposed the establishment of a mission. They were all pleased with the idea and declared their countrymen would be glad when one should be established.

The movement began in Constantinople. The city, a description of which will be found in a chapter devoted exclusively to that subject, has over 1,200,000 inhabitants. The majority are Turks, but the Armenians are next in number, there being over 150,000 of them. In 1831, when Rev. William Goodell was called from Malta (where he was engaged in missionary work) to Constantinople, there were about 100,000 Armenians in the city offering a very attractive field for effort. This was in June, 1831, but scarcely had he established himself in Pera, one of the suburbs of the city, when a destructive fire necessitated the removal of the mission to a town some few miles up the Bosphorus. Although thus meeting with adversity, the original purpose of the mission was not allowed to suffer, and in the following year we again find Mr. William Goodell in Constantinople, this time accompanied by two more efficient workers, Messrs. H. G. O. Dwight and W. G. Schauffler, both Americans. These three men of God were welcomed very cordially by the Patriarch, and were allowed to suffer no inconvenience that could be alleviated. It, indeed, seemed as though the mission was blessed of God. We will see later on how the Patriarch maintained his first attitude.

In our chapter on the Armenian Church, we have described at length its services and forms of worship. It was the policy of the missionaries from the inauguration of their work to leave severely alone the outer bulwarks of the Church, for this would only have instigated intense opposition from all quarters. It was thought best to transform first the spiritual, and that being changed, the outward manifestation in material forms and ceremonies would be done away with as a logical result.

That this method was a success was soon seen, and the first fruits of labor were very encouraging. In the year of the starting of the mission, Mr. Goodell during a visit was the means of converting two priests. It will be interesting to note that six years afterwards, when visiting the same place, sixteen were found who were believed to be earnest converts. In Broosa, too, where a mission had been established, the work was progressing finely. The first converts meant much for the cause, for they were two young teachers of influential positions, having under their tutorship many young people. But despite all hopes, this tranquility was not destined to continue long, and opposition very soon began to molest the workers. At Erzroom and at Trebizond, two mission stations of the American Board, outrages were continually perpetrated.

The Patriarch, heretofore so kindly to all mission enterprises, fearing that the movement meant an encroachment upon the National Church, declared himself in word and deed against it. In the year 1837, Patriarchal bulls were repeatedly issued threatening anathemas against all who should be found guilty of associating with missionaries or reading literature circulated by them. The Patriarch at Constantinople at that time was almost of Papal power and influence. He banished a number of Protestants from the Capital, imprisoned many and threatened to exile the missionaries, when the war between the Sultan and Mohammed Ali interfered, attracting the minds of the people to more serious problems. While we sadly lament this action of the Patriarch, we have no doubt as to his conscientiousness. He was, as he thought, protecting his people; for since the State had fallen, the

Church remained as the only bulwark of a distinctive nationality, and his fears were not ill-founded if the past is to be taken into account. Years before, the Roman Church had materially weakened the Armenian by proselyting large numbers of her members. Was the present measure, then, injudicious? We believe not.

Let us consider, too, that conservatism is the distinctive characteristic of all Oriental Christians. Ritualism, in vogue for ages, becomes sacred from use. It cannot be denied that for centuries the conservative ritualism of the Armenian Church was a bulwark of defence against Roman and Greek heresies. The severe animosity and antagonism existing between the Eastern and Western churches is an apt illustration of the Armenian Church as well. During the siege of Constantinople by the Turks, united forces of all Christians against Mohammedans was desirable, and to this end the Papal legate was to conform the reunion of Christendom at St. Sophia. Even at this critical moment the fiery protest rose in unison with Patriarch Gennadius from all Grecian lips, "Give us Sultan's turban rather than Cardinal's hat." It is easy to imagine if this was the feeling between cognate churches, what the feeling against a church which is altogether foreign and strange would be.

Things slowly came to a crisis; the methods of persecution were many and divers. Superstitious reports of the most absurd nature were circulated everywhere and believed, until the whole Church, with but few exceptions, changed its front to the offensive. Although in the year 1843 the Sultan, urged by Sir Stratford Canning and others, had ordered that no person should be persecuted for his religious opinions in the empire, anathemas and excommunications were repeatedly issued and produced their dire effects upon the minds of the people. With excommunication came social degradation and disgrace; the accursed one was excluded from home and relations, the bakers were forbidden to sell to him, and he was confined in prison. The terrible cruelties practiced upon the Christians in the three years following would take volumes to adequately relate. Many were the heroic souls who, still inspired with zeal, remained steadfast through the storm of conflict. The culmination of it all was the formation in 1846 of the first Armenian Evangelical Church.

However, before we enter into a detailed account of this, we propose to present a short sketch of a factor which all these years had exercised no little power as an auxiliary to the more strictly religious work. Missionaries soon discovered that if the presenting of Christianity were accompanied by educational work, much more tangible good would be accomplished. Accordingly, from almost the very outset, schools were established at nearly every mission station; thus the education of the intellect kept pace with the higher education of the heart. These are the handmaids of civilization.

The school that probably has had the most influence in this formative and unsettled epoch was that established at Constantinople in 1827. Indirectly the school had its origin in a farewell letter written by Jonas King, a manuscript copy of which was sent to some influential Armenians in the capitol. By this letter conviction came that reformation was necessary, and the institution referred to was founded with an eminent and learned man, Peshtimaljian, at its head.

We will not speak at length of the valuable services of this school of the mission, suffice it to say that six years later fifteen of its graduates were ordained as priests, one of them, Dere Kevork, being immediately placed at the head of another new school in the same city that had just been founded by both Turks and Armenians. Had it not been for the earnest work of the missionaries, it is doubtful whether this school would have ever come into existence.

The educational work increased in power and scope, and the following year, 1834, a high school was located at Para. Its principal was a very consecrated young man by the name of Hohannes Sahakian, who had been a short time before a student at Constantinople. While there a New Testament had fallen into his hands, and as a result he became an earnest Christian and gave some very valuable assistance in translation work at the mission. His companion, Senakerim, a teacher in the palace of the Patriarch, was converted about the same time, and also labored in a school for children at one of the stations.

But even the schools received their share of the general persecution, and as a result of the interference of the Vicar of the Armenian Patriarch, the High School at Pera was compelled to stop its work. However, the result was not wholly evil, for another was immediately started at Hasskioy by a rich banker, with Sahakian as superintendent and Der Kevork as one of its teachers. Although this school, with an attendance of over six hundred, was recognized by the Armenian Synod and made a national institution, it was done away with the following year because of certain threatenings made by a number of hostile bankers.

The work at Smyrna was significant for a remarkable advance in a world where women are esteemed of little importance. Here a female seminary was opened, and owing to the urgent appeal of an influential citizen, besides tendering back the former aid proffered by the mission, soon became self-supporting. The influence of the school, with an attendance of about forty at the outset, cannot be estimated.

Another important educational institution was the Seminary at Bebek, a theological school, in which, besides a critical study of the Bible, were taught Latin, Greek and Hebrew.

As we mentioned before, it was not the object of the missionaries to attack the outworks of the national church, nor to found a separate body. From the first, they, along with the converted numbers, objected very seriously to being known by the designation "Protestants," or any other name that would apear as an indication of disunion

However, as persecution became more and more intense, it was apparent that something must be done, and when in June, 1846, an anathema was issued excommunicating all who adhered to the new faith, nothing was left but to form a separate organization. Accordingly, in the following month, a meeting was called at Constantinople, at which the missionaries were present, and, after the reading of a covenant to which all assented, the First Evangelical Armenian Church became a reality. What was intended to be only missionary work spiritualizing the formalism of a nominally Christian church, thus resulted in the organization of a separate religious institution. To whatever causes we may attribute this division, they will not alter the fact that is was a sad and disadvantageous occurrence. This body at first numbering forty souls, of which three were women, was presided over by one of the former students of the Peshtimaljian school, a man entirely worthy of the trust. The initiatory thus being taken, other churches were almost immediately organized in other parts of the country. In two years there was a very strong church at Aintab, which grew to a membership of two hundred and sixty-eight in a few years, and others at Trebizord, Erzroom and Morsovan, among the first missionary stations, and also at Nicomedia and Adabazer. Although the aggregate membership at this time was not over a thousand, it meant much as a beginning.

We must not neglect to speak here of one of the leading benefactors of the new movement, Sir Stratford Canning, through whose untiring efforts concession after concession was made until the Protestant community enjoyed almost the same measure of tolerance as the National Church.

In the treaty of Paris, with the voluntary assent of the Sultan, these rights were incorporated and religious liberty was thus more fully insured. Free schools were organized to the number of thirty-eight, and the work progressed and widened in territory until it was found necessary to divide the field of labor. The Southern Mission, afterwards called the Central, was organized in 1856, and the Northern was again divided into the Eastern and Western Mission in 1860.

As the work progressed it was a source of great satisfaction to see native preachers gradually taking places as efficient pastors of the native congregations. They were rarely if ever compelled to call on the missionaries for help, as nearly all the churches managed, by a sacrifice on the part of both pastor and people, to be self-supporting from the beginning. Revivals became frequent and were the means of the conversion of many. In 1856 occurred a soul-stirring revival in Morsovan, my native town. The theological seminary at Bebek, not far from the capital, experienced a similar awakening, as also did Cæsarea and numbers of smaller cities.

Through the translation of Messrs. Goodell and Schauffler, the work received a new impulse. The former, with the aid of an Armenian, put forth a translation of the Bible in Turko-Armenian, that is, the Turkish language written in Armenian. The latter performed a similar service

THE EVANGELICAL CHURCH.   129

for the Turks, his translation being in their own language as written in the sacred characters.

Although these translations lent a wonderful impetus to the work in 1874, it was deemed necessary to appoint a revision committee, who six years later put forth an excellent version, written in both the Armenian and Turkish letters.

It would be useless in a short sketch of this kind to give a detailed account of the individual work of missionaries, although we fain would do so. We must be satisfied with touching upon the more important events. We cannot pass by, however, without some notice of associations and unions that came into being about this time as a result of the constantly increasing number of members of churches.

Organization is necessary to systematic work, and in 1857 the churches at Nicomedia, Adabazar and Bardizag formed themselves into what was known as the Bithyan Association.

A much larger and more important organization was the Union of the Evangelical Armenian Churches of Bithinia, now embracing twelve churches and stations. This was formed in 1864. The next year the Harpoot Evangelical Union came into existence, a union that did much in the promulgation of the gospel among the Armenians living in the wild region of the Koords, some little distance from Diarbekir. Other potent organizations were the Central and Cilicia Unions, formed at a later date. The results of these various associations were essentially good. Besides putting the church in closer contact and sympathy with each other, they learned to rely more upon themselves, and calls for aid from foreign countries became more and more infrequent.

Nor must it be supposed that the work of evangelization was confined to the Evangelical Church alone, for many members of the old National Church, who were essentially Protestants, effected many needed reforms. One of their measures was the publication of a new prayer book, which, though never used to any extent, created much interest and comment. No less encouraging was the fact that in the dissemination of the Scripture, numbers of copies of the New Testament were disposed of to Mohammedans, which, though undoubtedly bought for mere curiosity, could not fail to have some influence for good.

Within the last thirty-five years, although the growth of the Church has been marvelous, its causes cannot be said to have been entirely without disturbing influences. Calamity came in the shape of a dire famine, which prevailed in all Asia Minor during the years 1874 and 1875. At this time thousands wandered about the streets of Marsovan and other cities, begging bread from door to door. A large number died from famine, while some gratefully received aid from the missionaries at Cæsarea and Marsovan. This kindness was not suffered to go unrewarded, for on account of it many opened their hearts to the words of the gospel. We must especially speak in terms of praise of, Revs.

Farnsworth and C. C. Tracy, who have done so much to relieve the general suffering.

Among institutions which are instrumental in the missionary work, the Bible house at Constantinople deserves special mention. Thousands of copies of Scriptures are published here in modern Armenia as well as in thirty other languages. They are quickly sold and read by people of various nationalities. Besides the Bible, there are published from this institution books, tracts and newspapers of a religious and educational character. While in Constantinople it always afforded me great pleasure to visit this noble edifice, enjoying the devotional services conducted there every Lord's day.

The progress and prosperity of educational work has been, and is, an inspiring fact. We have already alluded to its importance and have mentioned some of the earliest schools.

There are several educational institutions at my home, Marsovan, among them being Anatolia College, where I received my early training, there is also a theological seminary of no little repute. My former teacher, Rev. Geo. F. Herrick, D.D., an eminent Oriental scholar, and Rev. C. C. Tracy, are the founders and constant inspiration of Anatolia College. We have spoken of the Theological school at Bebek; others of a similar nature were founded soon afterwards in Marash, Mardin and Horfoot, the last named town being the location of Armenia College.

Aintab, where missionary work has been exceptionally

prosperous, is the site of the College of Central Turkey. But the institution of which Armenians may feel most proud is the well known Robert College, named after its financial founder, Christopher R. Robert of New York City. This college, located first in Bebek and afterwards at Hissor, is one of the best institutions of the kind in the world, being well equipped with excellent professors and enjoying the patronage of nearly every nationality. It was established in 1863, through the working influence of Rev. Dr. Cyrus Hamlin, an American, who has since been its constant inspiration. Of late years the prosperity of Christian work among Armenians has equalled the highest expectations.

The influence of the Protestants upon the Turks has been salutary in its powers, and the latter are to-day held in higher esteem by them than ever. The young men are taking increasing interest in the Church, and a number of Young Men's Christian Associations have been organized. And by no means the least blessing is the advancement of woman from her degradation to a plane of culture and refinement, chiefly owing to the liberality of the natives themselves in the cause of female education. What a happy result that youths of both sexes share alike the opportunities of culture!

Prospects were never brighter. The number and rolls in the Evangelical churches are larger than ever before, and the common school system is one that shadows forth great results in the introduction of civilization. One hundred

THE EVANGELICAL CHURCH. 133

and fifty Evangelical churches have been established. Out of forty thousand Protestants in Asia Minor, thirty thousand are Armenians, because they have been selected as the first fruits of missionary effort for their ready appreciation of the Bible as the Word of God. Thus far the work of missionaries in the country have been restricted to Armenians, Greeks, Bulgarians, and others of ancient Christian churches. No Turks or Mohammedan tribes of any large number have been converted.

With hands ever upraised towards heaven, and with heart ever yearning for the better life, Armenia patiently awaits the day which cannot be far distant, when with uplifted head she may take her rightful place among her greater sisters and share their honor and respect.

HINDRANCES IN THE WORKING FORCES OF MISSIONS.*

There are in foreign fields serious problems yet unsolved, overlooking, however, numerous external difficulties. Denominationalism, I venture to affirm, is the gigantic obstacle in the path of missionary progress. I have seen and felt many times, while in my native country, the evil of sectarianism, which has often proved fatal to the incipient church.†

---

*From an address delivered by the author before the minister's meeting of Cleveland and vicinity in the First M. E. Church, Cleveland, O., Nov. 20, 1893.

†Besides those of the American Board whom we have mentionee, various minor denominational missions have been introduced in the country. Rev. G. S. Shishmanian, an Armenian educated in the Bible

Denomination after denomination brings to our people its peculiar dogma, each in bitter opposition to the other and each claiming the orthodox doctrine. Whom shall our people believe? Which one is right? How shall the infant religious mind of an Oriental grasp the truth amid such diverse representation? How natural for him to reason: truth does not contradict itself, therefore I reject all as false. He learns of Protestantism as possessing over two hundred divisions and sub-divisions, each teaching a different doctrine and plan of salvation. All this he can not understand, and is unwilling as an honest man to say that he believes in the doctrine or "articles of faith" of any one of them, until he has looked at all sides and studied every doctrine and article with care. And this he will not do. We ought to see to the solution of this problem without delay. We ought to right ourselves before we endeavor to right others. As I have had the pleasant opportunity of speaking from various pulpits, I have consulted the prominent clergymen of Protestant denominations concerning their opinion of Christian Unity. I am satisfied that they see the evils of division, and uniformly

---

school at Lexington, Ky., was sent to the Turkish capital in 1879 by the Disciples of this country. In 1884 he was followed by the Rev. Garabed Kevorkian, M. D., who made Marsova (one of the most important missionary stations of the American Board) the center of his operations. Disciples have five hundred and eighty-three communicants and a few common schools. Rev. Kaprilian, formerly a pastor of the Congregational churches in Nicomdia and Constantinople, now represents the Baptists. Dr. Dobrasiian was sent by the Friends of England to Constantinople as a medical missionary.

favor the idea of union, but no steps have been taken toward an organic union. We can never accomplish the cherished purpose by merely having so-called union in spirit, while divided in body. There is no perfect union in a spirit without an organic union—no unity in diversity. If there was a true spiritual union, it would manifest itself in the visible organization. Christ speaks of one flock and one shepherd. Conceive of a flock scattered and separated from the main herd and grazing on hills remote from one another. If we are all near the Divine Shepherd, we are not far from one another.

As I study the history of denominations, I am astonished to find upon what small matters divisions have been made, and feel that mere opinion has been given undue prominence, while weightier matters have been neglected.

A foreigner finds a few denominations whose creeds are so nearly alike that they seem to love one another and work together in comparative harmony, or who have lost the spirit of controversy in the spirit of Christ. But he is daily disgusted in finding such great diversity of feeling and belief, especially in the country districts, and in hearing unkind disputes on religious questions, and thrusts at one another from gospel pulpits. A foreigner, so bewildered, is led to decide that if there ever was a true religion it has been lost. Christ realized this danger when he prayed that those who believed on him might "be one." Said He, "As thou, Father, art in me, and I in Thee, that they also may be one in us: that the world may believe that

Thou hast sent me." (John XVII., 21). The world, as a whole, never will believe that Christ is our head until we are one in doctrine as well as in spirit, and in name as well as in doctrine. There is no reason in flattering ourselves that we are thus united in spirit and teaching, for when that happy day dawns—as it will, for Christ prayed for it—we will not differ in our faiths.

God and Christ do not differ in doctrine or plan, and we are to be one as they are one. St. Paul appreciated this, for he wrote to the Corinthians: "I beseech you, brethren, by the name of our Lord Jesus Christ, that ye will speak the same thing, and that there be no divisions among you; but that ye be perfectly joined together in the same mind and in the same judgment (I. Cor. I, 10). But, not understanding the prayer of Christ and the teaching of Paul, some will argue that these divisions are necessary in order to the rapid spread of the gospel. They tell us this competition is essential to rapid growth. It is well to remember that rapid growth is not always strong growth. It is better to have the spirit in accord with God's Word and grow more slowly at first, than to have the rapid growth through rivalry, which will weaken the very bodies it builds, and pollute with eternal tumult the Spirit of Christ.

"Let nothing be done through strife or vain glory." (Phil. II., 3.) Others will argue that men are differently constituted, and all these different creeds are necessary to lay hold of the different orders of mind and to take them all to heaven; that, in short, when God conceived His plan of salvation He was not wise enough to make one that would save all who should accept it; therefore, we mortals must change it and add to it by our superior wisdom, or God's plan will prove a failure. God's plan of salvation is a unity. There are no divisions or sub-divisions in it. It is His plan, and no man or set of men, however wise, powerful or good, have the right to add to it or take from it. Remember the everlasting doom of which St. John writes, in the conclusion of the inspired Word, to him who "adds or takes away" from the words of the sacred book. (Rev. xxii., 18-19.)

If our human creeds and dogmas were like God's Word they would not contradict one another, as God is in harmony with Himself in all His works. If any of them are taught as the oracles of God they are positively wrong in their tests of fellowship, for the Bible should be our standard. Every man has a right to his own creed, written or unwritten, but he has no right, under Christ, to refuse fellowship to those who do not see altogether as he does, nor to retain or uphold such creed when he finds it is opposed to the plain teachings of Christ. Denominationalism discriminates in giving that love which is due to all men. It engenders strife between friends and neighbors and hinders mutual edification. "I am a Methodist, he is a Presbyterian; what do I care? Let him suffer," or "let his own denomination take care of him." How mean the narrowness and bigotry of intolerable sectarianism! Such a feeling practically severs the tender relationship of the

Fatherhood of God and the universal brotherhood of man, which Christ had inspired and indellibly stamped on the hearts of His disciples. "As I have loved you, so also love one another." Does this commandment give boundaries or discriminations, or does it mean that Christ loved the Methodist and rejected the Presbyterian? We all say no; yet how natural for denominationalism to foster such bitter feelings.

The question arises often in my mind: If Christ should revisit the earth, which one of these denominations would he join? If he would unite with one of them, what a shock would seize the rest, who uniformly claim Him as the supreme head of their church! I do not suppose Christ either would or could encourage sectarianism—He who so ardently prayed His Father that His disciples "may be one." His Word ever teaches, "be of the same mind." How could He practice diversity and division? One thing I am sure Christ would do. He would demolish all our denominational lines and confirm the reunion of the primitive faith. Then let us who are "ambassadors of Christ" be actuated by the same principle of unity and peace, and may it be our firm conviction to put into operation the organic forces of a united church.

It is said that one of our Armenian poets had a vision, in which he found himself confronting St. Peter at the portals of heaven. After stating from whence he came, the following conversation ensued. Said our good friend:

"While on earth I was an earnest member of an

Armenian National church; tell me, O Saint, are there any of my Illuminiterians* here?"

"I know of none," answered St. Peter.

"None!" echoed the questioner with much surprise; then recovering himself, "there are Baptists here?"

"No Baptists."

"Any Congregationalists?"

"None, my friend."

"Are there any Methodists?"

"No Methodists."

"There must be some Presbyterians?"

"There are no Presbyterians here."

"And no Roman Catholics?"

"Heaven contains no Roman Catholics; no, not one."

"Pray, great father," said the pilgrim, much bewildered, "if there are no Illuminiterians, no Baptists, no Congregationalists, no Methodists, no Presbyterians, nor Catholics, what people may enter your beautiful city?"

"Ignorant one, listen! Countless thousands from your world stand before the throne singing praises to God and the Lamb. Hark! you can faintly hear their voices now. Soon shall you stand with that blessed multitude. But know thou that neither Methodist, nor Baptist, nor any other such enter the kingdom of heaven; we bear but one name hear, significant and glorious; henceforth thou shall be known as "Christian," for of such are all the Celestial City."

*This name is used by the Armenians for the Armenian Church.

With these words St. Peter ceased speaking and the vision departed.

This story, though simple, brings us face to face with truth. Christ is the center of union, "Christian" must be the converging lines. No ray emenating from the Son of Righteousness can be called by any other name than that which is derived from its source. This is the one word uniting all denominations, and it is the watchword for all future attempts at final unity. It points at once to the foundation of our hope. It is significant of the greatest and dearest name ever known by mortals. It is an appellation hallowed by the associations of centuries. The name "Christian" suggests to us the fagot, the gibbet and the sword. It brings with it the echoes of heroic defense, the single voice distinguished above all the controversies of the multitude. It seems to waft to our ears from inland Africa, from India and from China, the pleading prayers and earnest words of self-sacrificing ones, whom to call by any other title would be to dishonor.

The Lord's redeemed have not yet learned their universal language, and there is much misunderstanding as a result. Let the name "Christian" ever remain in the simple God-language, and may its associations of blessings and of hope increase throughout all the years of conquest over wrong.

St. Paul directs a letter "unto the Church of the Thessalonians in God the Father and in the Lord Jesus Christ." His first epistle is addressed to "All in Rome, beloved of

God, called saints." The second and third "To the Church of God at Corinth," the fourth to the "Churches of Galatia," the fifth to the "Saints at Ephesus and Faithful in Christ Jesus," the sixth to the "Saints at Phillippi with the Bishops and Deacons." We learn from all this : First, that in the days of the apostles, the assemblies of Christians in a given region were the Church of that religion as the Churches of Galatia and Asia; sometimes Churches of God, sometimes Churches of Christ (Rom. xvi., 16); sometimes Churches of the Saints (I. Cor. xiv., 33). Second, That the Christians in every city constituted the Church of that city (as the Church of Corinth and Ephesus), with no denominational divisions as now; simply Churches of God, Churches of Christ.

It is very plain, therefore, that the church, in the New Testament sense, is a divine institution, resting upon divine authority, and having divine claims upon us. It is a church "In God the Father and the Lord Jesus Christ." It follows, then, that the spiritual ties that bind such a body together are a common faith, hope, love and submission to the same divine will.

What folly to name such a church after a man, an ordinance or a human system! No man or company of men, however wise, good or great, have the right to dictate the terms of membership in a church of God. It is purely and only a divine right. Then let us cast aside those non essential things which separate us, and aim towards a final reunion of God's people on God's ground. We cannot unite on your ground or mine, but on God's ground. The faith he taught was not in human doctrine, but in a personal Saviour. Said he: "This is my beloved Son, hear ye Him."

John did not write his gospel to teach doctrine, but he distinctly says: "These are written that ye might believe that Jesus is the Christ, the Son of God; and that believing ye might have life through His name." (John xx., 31).

Peter preached upon the day of Pentecost: "This Jesus hath God raised up, whereof we all are witnesses." (Acts ii., 32).

If the Christians of to-day would obey the commandments and take the Bible in its purity and simplicity, there would be an end to all controversies and troubles in missionary fields. Our denominationalism is not the gospel. A thousand million souls are, in this age of enlightenment, in utter darkness, without hope and without Christ. This great number, however, does not include those in Christian lands who have not yet accepted Christ, but the people who are ignorant of Him.

One thousand millions! Bear in mind your personal responsibility to this vast multitude of unsaved, and, as clever business men, reason promptly what is the wise course to take to hasten the spiritual welfare of this vast multitude. Remember, too, that as the work of Gospel dissemination has been slow in the past, to follow in the future a somewhat different course would be wise. Our spiritual forces have been divided. Let us unite then, let us unite our finances; union is strength; divided forces can not hail the victory. Let us concede, as brethren, the non-essential, and unite fully upon the essential at home and abroad. Let our motto be: "In Christ unity, in opinion liberty, and in all things charity."

During the days of the Apostles the only term of membership and test of fellowship was belief in Christ and strict obedience to Him as the declared Son of God.

It is so simple that a child can understand it, and so wise that the deepest mind will not despise it. This, God's ground of belief in and obedience to a personal Savior, is the only possible ground upon which His children can and must unite. When we do so:

First. We will save an immense amount of money now foolishly spent in small towns to keep in existence many weak churches in place of giving full support and life to one strong one.

Second. We will heed the instructions of Paul.

Third. We will answer the prayers of Christ.

Fourth. We will show a united front to the enemy and the world will believe in our Saviour.

Fifth. We will promote the spirit of harmony, the spirit of love, the spirit of God.

Sixth. We will glorify Christ instead of the parties to which we belong.

Seventh. We will carry to a logical conclusion the present movements of Christian Endeavorers, Young Men's Christian Associations, Young Women's Christian Associations, Kings Sons and Daughters, and other kindred organizations.

Eighth. We will stand uncondemned before Him, who is the author of the only sure and harmonious plan of salvation.

We do not look to Christ enough and are too much inclined to follow men. St. Paul once discovered that tendency in the Church of Corinth, and listen to the rebuke he gave them: "Every one of you saith, I am of Paul, and I am of Apollos and of Cephas, and I of Christ. Is Christ divided? Was Paul crucified for you? or were ye baptized in the name of Paul?" (1 Cor. i., 12-13). He gave them to understand that the "preaching of the cross" was the power of God (18 v.), and besought them to be of one mind (10 v.). The question that united them was: " Who is for Christ?" and it is the one that must unite us all to-day. We are saying, if not by our lips, at least by our actions, "I am for Knox, I for Calvin, I for Wesley, I for Luther, I for Swedenborg, I for Campbell." No injustice to these imperial names, but is Christ divided? Was Knox crucified for us, or were we baptized in the name of Campbell? No, no; we will not be chained to the cemeteries of the past, although those who are buried in them were great men of God. We prefer to look to Christ, the "Author and Perfector of our faith." Let us then take our theology not from the graveyards of the past ages, but from the open tomb of a risen Christ.

GLIMPSES OF SOCIAL LIFE.

"Zealous, yet modest; 'tho' free;
Patient of toil; serene amidst alarms;
Inflexible in faith; invincible in arms."
—*Beattie.*

THE Orient has never lost its power of fascination, because it has practically never lost its old manners and customs. Its people seem incapable of overcoming their centuries-rooted veneration for old customs, which dominates them with a stronger power than the scepter of kings.

Allow me now to extend to you, my reader, a cordial invitation to pass over the threshold of an Armenian home and to spend a few hours within our family circle. They are all deeply interested in your bright country and people, and I am sure, in turn, you would find much to interest you in our country's customs and manners, so old and romantic. As the morning light first touches the mountain tops, so our glimpses of home life begin with the higher classes. Journeying together under Oriental skies, we will find striking contrasts everywhere between Armenian and Turkish homes. Home is a magic word. There is a predominating love, the sunshine of happiness, harmony and beauty in the homes of the Armenians. No matter how old it may be in fashion or how simple in decoration, no human language can ever express the deep remembrances in the heart of an Armenian far away from its ties. It captures the lonely soul with a thrill, on the wings of happy and loving recollections. It is something tender, yet full of inspiration, that fills one with the memories of sweet home!

As we are wending our way homeward, you will find to your great astonishment the narrow and zig-zag streets— running from everywhere to nowhere—so thronged with dogs, horses, donkeys, and sometimes with long trains of supercilious camels and buffalo *arabas*, that you have to challenge everything and every being for the right of way. Above all, you will have a lively time with the reputed Turkish dogs; fortunately in the portions of the country where Europeans dwell, they have nearly disappeared from the streets. Those you meet are civilized and respectful to Mohammedan and Christian alike, while the old breed would howl at a Christian but remain quiet when a Turk passed that way. Even the dogs are getting civilized, which is more than can be said of the bipeds of the slums.

Of the defunct dogs, we may say the red-coats were their assassins, and loaded walking-sticks the weapons used in the night. An English sea-rover vowed he would kill a dog every night when returning to ship from his games. He kept his word and more, for when unlucky at cards he would dispatch two or three curs in ambling down the hill. Ere long dogs were scarce on his route. To be sure he would not miss a victim, he took the narrow side streets. A fellow friendly to dogs—of course a Turk—waylaid the Briton and, with some assistance, sent him to his berth, a battered specimen of humanity.

Besides the dogs, you may meet here and there a careless, lazy-looking set of vagabonds on the corners sunning themselves. They are the tramps of the town, or next to them—absolutely good-for-nothing, unmitigated nuisances, who have no excuse for their existence, except the fact that they were born. Their motto seems to be, "Grab and eat as much as you can and whine." They do nothing but rest themselves, anywhere, everywhere, all day and every day. They are lucky if they can get ahead of some wandering dogs in securing the best shaded corner where they may stretch their lazy bones in peace. They always laugh at the wrong thing, at the wrong place, in the wrong time. To do nothing, to be of no earthly use, seems to be the keynote of their happy life. "Consider the lilies of the field, how they grow; they toil not, neither do they spin." These tramps must be the lilies of the swamp! Fruit sellers, Turkish grinders and *hamals*, or porters, are to be seen on every hand.

It adds a stranger aspect to the street scene to see the houses and yards, like castles or picturesque fortifications, surrounded by solid black walls from fifteen to twenty-five feet high, with a heavy stone gate before each house and an iron hammer suspended from its center. For admittance, the stranger must knock the hammer at the gate. Most of the residences are two-story houses, built of sun-dried brick around an open court-yard, and plastered within and without. There are few stone buildings and none of frame. Most of the houses have a balcony overlooking a tangled

A TURK GRINDER.

garden. Window ledges are abloom with flowers. The numerous small windows are closely latticed on the outside with net-work of iron bars arranged in pairs. The roofs of the houses are covered with tile. As a rule, the residences are built very close together, with a space between them of not more than six feet, so a distant view of the dwellings makes them compact-looking, as though erected one above the other.

As we enter within the gate, passing through the yard we come to the house. Before we enter, however, let us go to the rear of the building, where generally are gardens. Lofty trees surround the house, with their branches of the brightest green; sparkling fountains play in the rich sunshine; flower beds, exquisite in variety of hue, with shrubs and roses, greet the eye on all sides. The air is freshened with soft zephyrs and sweetened with roses. There the nightingale builds his little nest in the bush. Oh, how often the bright days of my youth opened with the melodious songs of that delicate bird! How often our sunrise prayers and songs of hallelujah from our family altars, mingling with the soft strains, were wafted by the morning breeze before the throne of God! How precious the remembrances of the dreamlike sweetness of home, which still rest on my soul like solemn shadows! As we enter our house you will meet with a most cordial reception from the household, for hospitality and kindness to strangers is the first law in the Orient—a most pleasing and characteristic feature of Armenian society. The kind words and eager and ready display of hospitality, all vieing with one another in supplying your wants, is a striking scene to an American. Indeed, our people are the most friendly of friends. They enjoy life because they make other people enjoy it. Home is a philanthropic institution with them, so much so that some regret the introduction of western ideas, which has led to the founding of asylums, hospitals and orphanges, since custom will not allow a stranger within the gates to suffer from lack of food or shelter. He is given a seat at the table, and to sup with the master of the house means to lodge with him. The host furnishes slippers and night-robes. The guest is expected to entertain all callers with some account of himself, his country, its laws and religion, manners and customs. Interchange of visits is always expected. The people love to congregate, and greatly enjoy meeting together. In Christian homes, men and women meet in the reception room, but generally ladies, gentlemen and children form separate groups and chat on general topics. The themes vary according to the social position and intelligence of the company. If a Turkish house, it possesses two apartments—the *haremlik* and *selamlik*. The former is the ladies' reception room, and the latter for gentlemen. Holidays and long winter evenings are usually devoted to a pleasant and ancient pastime, which is indeed one of the happiest features of Oriental life. The master of the house opens the door of his home and welcomes the guest with numerous expressive gestures of unbounded hospitality. In the immediate entrance of the house there is a paved space; here custom and etiquette demands the people to remove their shoes instead of their fez before entering the rooms, while the hats, like the bonnets of American ladies, are never taken off, within or without the house. After exchanging graceful salutations, inquiries after each other's health, and formal civilities, the guest is ushered into a cheery court, thence into the reception room, where the first thing, coffee, is served, the universal beverage of the Levant. The square room, which they occupy, is comfortably fitted and arranged with a profusion of sofas, embroidered cushions and mattresses for sitting and reclining, and a few chairs, on a floor beautified by a fine display of rich Oriental rugs. In the center of the room is placed a stove, or a brazier, filled with a charcoal-made fire, as coal is not yet indispensable. The room is illumined by bright lamps, the old-fashioned tallow candle or olive-oil wick being long abandoned. Everything is agreeably prim and neat. The lady callers all cluster around the genial hostess, who sits by her babe singing soft and low the sweet, simple, cradle song, while the men are engaged in a discussion of the current events. They often exchange remarks with the ladies. The young boys have a lively time by themselves; they are eagerly planning upon the morrow to have a game in the field, or contemplating to engage in some sort of mischief, as is the characteristic of all boys. Little girls, with rosy faces, are clustered with their dolls and kittens around the good old grandmother, who tells them riddles and amusing stories, while the long, white-whiskered patriarch, bowed with years and honors, tells of his first flirtation, or of the social or municipal changes wrought in the country during his day. The remarks of the venerable man are always interesting, as revealing the evolution of the times. The house servant is on duty with such functions as arranging the shoes in pairs, that the guests may easily find them when departing. After games and conversation, the happy company indulge in cigarettes, coffee, sweetmeats and *narghile*, or the flexible rosewater pipe, much similar to the *hookah* of Hindoostan. It is always filled with shiraz tobacco. Time wears pleasantly on, the guests are sure to depart late, and most always with the satisfaction of having had an enjoyable time.

In many Armenian homes pianos and organs are coming into use, but are not yet indispensable. Our young men play the flute with an exquisite touch. The old-fashioned bagpipe of the Orient is of peculiar construction. Made of sheepskin, with a small mouth-piece, the instrument is formed from a combination of cow-horn and three reeds, with holes in them. The dulcimer is of Oriental origin. As the prototype or substitute of the pianoforte, which has rendered melody in so many American homes, it has been of great service to the commercial interests of music. The music of the Orient is noted for a characteristic plaintiveness quite charming to the ear. This feature is scientifically explained as arising from a sort of minor, which can only have chords in octaves.

Now comes our dinner time! Would you not come with us, my reader? We will be delighted to have you accompany us to the table. I assure you our Armenian cuisine is suited to western palates. Our people well understand that a man's stomach is an easy avenue to his heart.

First, hands are washed in running water. All are seated around the table of brightly-polished brazen platter, with neatly folded napkins, and spoons of box-wood and tortoise shell by the side of each. Soup comes first; then *pilav*, a dish resembling porridge; then meat, cooked in various styles of Oriental culinary art, bearing a close resemblance to that of France. Wines prized as the very best are continually to be found on the table. Lambs are roasted whole, in Homeric fashion; then olives, cheese and fruit are served. Thus dish follows dish, from everlasting to everlasting. Lastly come *chibouk*, delicate sweetmeats from Smyrna and Scio, and coffee, which is sipped out of cups not larger than the shell of the Maderia nut. On festival occasions we have plates of some rare delicacy.

My dear reader, our Orientals are not only differentiated from others by certain features of physical type and by language, but in ideas and modes of thinking as well.

Among the low and ignorant, where popular education is of a meagre sort, superstition has full sway—especially among the Turks. Many of them are amusing to strangers. Orientals, however, believe in them as firmly as they do in religion. For instance, they deem it a serious matter to be the victim of an evil eye. Fortunately, a remedy has been invented for every emergency—for the evil eye a word from the Koran, or garlic, taken internally, are antidotes. Dog bread is used as a charm; blue beads on horses, donkeys and buffaloes are charms against the malice of the envious and evil-eyed. That nothing must be wasted that can be used as food by dogs or fish, is a superstition tending to promote economy. You bring bad luck by entering a harem with the right foot. There are, in their imaginations only, creatures of dim, unspeakable shapes, from the regions of hell, that horrify them in darkness.

Some days are unlucky. The Sultan will postpone an interview if it falls on an unlucky day. Sometimes a long-forgotten and lost grave of a saint suddenly becomes a reputed centre of supernatural performances. Some one, no matter who, tells his neighbors that while crossing the grave of a certain saint his disease at once departed from him. No one knew before whether the grave was of a saint or Satan, or whether the originator of the report is worthy of confidence or not. The story goes with lightning speed, bringing in throngs the sick and the diseased from remotest parts to the mound of the would-be supernatural dead. What a strange yet pathetic scene to see the poor victims of superstition and illness kissing the stones and the dust of the graves with fervent supplications and vows!

When at home, I scorned and laughed at such odd spectacles, with a sense of mingled contempt and pity; but since I have seen American throngs about the fortune-teller, I cherish somewhat merciful feelings toward our Oriental nuisance.

STORIES.

In common with other Orientals, the Turks are fond of stories. Many good ones are current among the people and nearly all have a moral to them. Nasr-ed-din-Hoja is an ideal hero or victim of many Hunchausen tales. This teacher and notorious wag is supposed to live in Bagdad. I am tempted to relate several stories concerning him. I am indebted to Hon. Samuel S. Cox, the late American Minister to Turkey, for the translation of the following stories:

A belated beggar knocks at the Hoja's door.

"What do you want," he called down from an upper window.

"Come down, good Hoja, and I will tell you," replies the mendicant.

Having descended and opened the front door, the beggar asked for alms.

"Come up stairs," said the Hoja, and the mendicant was taken to the top floor.

"I am sorry, poor man," said the Hoja, "but I have no alms for you."

"Why did you not tell me so at the door?" inquires the beggar angrily.

"Why did you not tell me what you wanted before I came down?" retorts the Hoja.

* * *

One day the Hoja is too lazy to preach his usual sermon at the Mosque. He simply addresses himself to the congregation, saying:

"Of course you know, O faithful Mussulmans, what I am going to say."

The congregation cry out with one voice:

"No, Hoja, we do not know."

"Then, if you do not know, I have nothing to say to you," replies the Hoja, and leaves the pulpit.

Next time he again addresses his congregation, saying:
"Know ye, O faithful Mussulmans, what I am going to say to you?"

Fearing that if, as on the previous time, they say "No," the Hoja would leave them again without a sermon, all cried:

"Yes, Hoja, we do know."

"Then if you do know what I am going to say," quietly remarked the Hoja, "of course, there is no need of my saying it." He again steps down from the pulpit, to the consternation of the congregation.

On the third time, the Hoja again puts his question:

"Know ye, O faithful Mussulmans, what I am going to preach to you?"

The congregation, determined not to be disappointed again, take counsel on the question. Accordingly some of them reply:

"No, Hoja, we do not know," while others cry:
"Yes, Hoja, we do know."

"Very well, then," says Hoja, "as there are some of you who do know, and others who do not know, what I am going to say, let those who do know, tell it to those who do not know," and quickly leaves the pulpit.

* * *

"Oh Hoja! When will the end of the world come?"

"Ask me something difficult; that is quite easy to answer," is the calm reply. "When my wife dies, it will be the end of half the world; when I die, it will be the end of the whole world."

* * *

Hoja was about to marry, and prepared to build a house. The good neighbors told him his wife would turn the house upside down. So he built it wrong side up, that it might be, when turned upside down, O. K.

Hoja borrows from a friend a large copper vessel, in which to do his washing. A few days afterward, the vessel is returned clean, washed and polished. Inside of it is another, but much smaller, copper vessel.

"What is this, Hoja?" asks his friend. "I lend you one vessel and you bring me back two!"

"It is very curious," said the Hoja. "It appears that your vessel, while in my possession, must have given birth to a baby vessel. Of course both belong equally to you."

"Oh, thank you, good Hoja," says the man, laughing, and without more parley agrees to receive back both vessels.

Some time after this the Hoja again applies for the loan of the large vessel—"the mother vessel," as he described it. The demand is readily granted. Before leaving, the Hoja inquires after the health of the "baby vessel." He expresses pleasure at hearing that it was doing extremely well.

A week, then a month elapses, but no Hoja appears to return the borrowed vessel. The proprietor, at length losing patience, goes himself to obtain it.

"Very sorry," says Hoja, "but your copper vessel is dead."

"Dead, Hoja!" cries the other in surprise; "What do you mean?"

"Just what I say," replies the Hoja; "your vessel is dead."

"Nonsense, Hoja!" says the man—irritated at the Hoja's quiet manner, "how can a copper vessel die?"

"Read up your natural history, my good friend," answers the imperturbable, puffing quietly at his long pipe, "and you will see that everything that gives birth to a child must inevitably succumb in due course to the fate of all mortals. You were willing enough to believe that your vessel had given birth to a 'baby vessel.' I do not see, therefore, why you should now doubt my word as to its being dead."

* * *

One night before retiring, Hoja said to his wife: "If it rain to-morrow, I shall go to my field; if it do not rain, I shall go to my vineyard."

"Say, if it please God, Hoja," suggested his wife.

"Whether it please God or not," replies Hoja, "I shall go to one or the other."

"Hoja," says his wife, "say, if it please God."

"Nothing of the kind," says Hoja; "I shall go."

Next day it is not raining, and Hoja starts to go to his vineyard. He has not gone far, however, when he is stopped by the king's troopers, who compel him to work all day in repairing the roads. It is quite late at night when he is set free. By the time he arrives at his house, every one is fast asleep. His wife, putting her head out of the window, asks who it is.

"Wife," replied Hoja, "if it please God, it is I."

* * *

A friend calls on Hoja to borrow his donkey.

"Very sorry," says Hoja, who does not want to lend the animal, "but the donkey is not here; I have hired him out for the day."

Unfortunately, just at that moment the donkey begins to bray loudly, thus giving the direct lie to the Hoja.

"How is this, Hoja?" says his friend, "you say the donkey is away, and here he is braying in the stable."

Hoja, nothing daunted, replies in a grave manner:

"My dear sir, please do not demean yourself so low as to believe the donkey rather than myself—a fellow man and a venerable Hoja with a long gray beard."

EDUCATION.

Compulsory education is unknown in Asia Minor. The government renders no assistance to non-Mohammedan schools. Each nationality has its own schools quite as distinct as its churches. The Protestants, however, make no distiction in their schools. Of the Armenian higher institutions and colleges, we have elsewhere spoken.

Mohammedanism teaches that secular education is subordinate to and dependent on religious instruction. So it was that all the schools of early times were attached to mosques, and under the direction of the *Ulema* or religious teacher. Sultan Orchan was conspicuous for the founding of schools and colleges. Secular education, independent of religious instruction, began in 1846. Those who complete the course of study in the higher schools are granted a degree and given a mastership in a primary school. Several years more of training are required of those who wish to be *Ulemas* or religious teachers in the mosques. Those who are most proficient in their studies are trained in the legal profession, for all Turkish law is founded on the Koran. The revenue for the support of this system of education is derived from the church lands of the empire.

National schools are to be found in all the principal cities. In Constantinople, for instance, Armenians alone have over fifty schools for both sexes, but many of the small villages are deprived of this blessing. The Mohammedan boy's entrance in school, at the age of seven, is a festive occasion. The whole school goes to the home of the lad, who is placed on a richly caparisoned donkey. Formed in double-file procession, they escort the young student to the school-house, singing songs. It is certainly a beautiful custom, which tends to impress on the minds of the young the importance of this new sphere of life. These Turkish common schools present a very singular scene to a stranger. The pupils are all seated cross-legged in semi-circular clusters around the hoja or teacher, in the porch of the mosque, on bare marble pavements. The hoja, as a rule, is an old man with white whiskers. He holds in his hand an extremely long stick, which reaches to all parts of the school, from one end to the other. As the hoja is quite old and too lazy to move from his seat, in case of mischief he stretches his unmerciful stick over the unruly ones. As he is asleep nearly half of the time, on opening his eyes he finds the entire school a lusty play and fighting ground of wild disorder. His long stick is now on duty to establish peace and order. I remember many true stories of how these young students got even with their patriarchal teacher in anointing his head and whiskers with oil and wax while he was in his usual sleep in the school room, and of what a hard time he frequently had in finding his stolen stick.

The strangest aspect of these Turkish schools is the manner of studying. All read their lessons aloud in shrill and deafening voices. All recite at the same time in a loud monotone. No wonder the old schoolmaster goes to sleep;

how could he find rest otherwise? When I passed by a mosque where these Turkish schools are held, I used to cover my ears. In the absence of desks, the writing is done by holding the paper in the left hand and writing from right to left.

THE FAIR SEX.

One of the most frequent questions asked me by the young people of this country is concerning the courtship and marriage of our Eastern youth. The frequency of this question has led me to conclude that this is the favorite theme of young American hearts.

Oriental harems have been the basis of many a delusive fiction. Their secluded privacy of indoor life has thrown about them the charm of mystery. Islamism does not allow women to appear in public save when they are closely veiled. Even at home their apartments are entirely separated from those to which male callers are admitted. For centuries the women of the harem, isolated from society, had no knowledge of the outside world, except what they saw in their limited field of observation, or heard from the men of their own household. In the mosque and in public conveyances, as at home, they are separated in special apartments. Aishe, Mohammed's wife, originated the custom of seclusion and thus the tradition and customs of centuries do not readily yield to innovation. The Arabic word "harem" is synonomous to the English "home." "Harem" means "secret," "forbidden," and if the Turks keep all their other secrets as closely as their wives, they would be possessing at least one virtue of real merit.

Turkish women sometimes disregard the law and escape in groups to shady nooks and glens, throw aside their veils and have a right good time when husbands are away. A Swiss traveller relates that in a narrow lane of Constantinople he met a Mohammedan lady so enrobed that he could see nothing of her but the tips of her fingers and glaring black eyes. As she was followed by female slaves, she looked about to see that none of the faithful were in sight, then pulled down her veil exposing a face of rare beauty, and laughed merrily at the surprise she had given a Christian as she passed on. Those alone are esteemed the upper ten of the Orient, or the model wives of the East, who are confined to their own homes, devoted to the care of their children, or engaged in sewing, knitting or decorating the rooms.

They find their reward in the refined comfort which they shed about them. Such as these are considered to give tone to the best Turkish families. Their conversation, when entertained, is peculiar yet interesting, and is of the practical kind which commands respect.

To an Oriental, outer pomp and glory, and visible attractions and charms are as nothing beside the little nestling home which with its "forbidden" beauties and fireside is the only centre of all his thoughts, pleasures, affections and life. Happy indeed is she who finds herself the one wife of an affectionate husband! The practice of polygamy by Mo-

"SWEETHEART."

hammedans is greatly exaggerated by many writers. Very few indeed can afford more than one wife.

Nothing could be more encouraging than the gradual disappearance of the custom. It has doubtless been the source of much unhappiness in the past and may be entirely abandoned in the near future. Whoever has reflected on the subject can understand that there can be no homelife worthy of the name, except where one woman reigns as queen.

A cloudy or stormy social atmosphere is not the kind in which to bring up children. Mohammed tolerated, but did not encourage or enjoy polygamy. The Koran says, "If ye fear that ye shall not act with equity towards orphans of the female sex, take in marriage of such other women as please you two, or three, or four, and not more."

What was intended as a favor to unfortunate females, proved the source of their undoing. The Prophet unquestionably had respect for women, as he owed his success largely to his wife.

The education of the Turkish women is limited to housekeeping of a respectable order, and the Oriental culinary art. For accomplishments she learns to dance, sing and play the dulcimer. It would not do to omit that in their fancy needle-work, rugs, drapery, etc., there is much to be admired; silk scarfs wrought in golden threads formed of love ballads from Hafiz, or sacred verses from the Koran; jewel-sprinkled cushions, richly ornamented robes and garments, indicate expert skill and good taste of fancy. Indeed their skill and devotion to this truly fine art might well be imitated elsewhere. In fact, a great many articles and furniture of the home are household industries.

Fondness for fine clothes they have in common with all other women. Their costumes conform to the latest western style, as fashions are introduced direct from the French capital. The purely indoor dress is simple yet rich in silk, velvet and satin. First an undergarment of light gauze material, with full and long sleeves; next baggy trousers of the zouave type of bright color. These are more or less concealed by the gold embroidered robe or outer garment, which is open in front and has slits at the sides of wide flowing sleeves. Such a costume is certainly a good one from a sanitary point of view. The zouave sleeveless vest is worn whenever weather or taste calls for it. The head dress is usually a velvet cap, decorated with tinsel and jewelry. Their arms and necks are literally loaded with silver and gold bracelets and necklaces set with costly stones. Their feet are encased in pointed-toed slippers, which turn up like a skate.

The Turkish wife or wives must not complain of illtreatment on peril of missing paradise or getting divorced. She must not frown on her husband; if her actions in any way displease him, she is in imminent danger, should she die before he is reconciled. Her duty is to court and obtain his good will. A wife whose tongue has made trouble for her husband will have that "useful" appendage lengthened to one hundred and fifty feet at the judgment! With such a weapon, what man would dare to marry one of them! The prophet himself declares, he would not officiate at the funeral of his own daughter if her husband was displeased with her.

The Armenian ladies, justly renowned for their beauty and fairness, though so close neighbors, radically differ from the Turkish in many particulars. Circumstances have been more propitious for Armenian women's advancement; seclusion, polygamy or divorce is unknown among them. They share alike with young men the advantages of culture and education. American customs, and furniture, pianos and sewing machines, bring repose and harmony in their homes. They entertain respectable callers of either sex, but take especial delight in the company of wives and daughters of European and American nobles and ambassadors. They read, write, dress in European fashion and are thus quite responsive to the evolution of the times. It must not be denied, however, that with all their modern accomplishments they are not permitted as much liberty, neither are they esteemed or valued quite so highly, as the women of America. It is a pleasure to mention that the rising generation of the Turkish ladies are indicating a slight tendency toward European progressiveness. Their *yeshmaks*, or veils, are getting decidedly thinner and thinner; some, indeed, so thin that, like a transparent glass, they shine out the beautiful countenance of the lady within. They are seeking the acquaintance of their European sisters, and are endeavoring to acquire their manners and customs as far as their religion will allow. The general diffusion of knowledge, however, like everything Turkish, is slow. National ignorance, superstition and bigotry are largely the result of uneducated mothers, and the uneducated mothers the result of the existing institutions or the absence of institutions. Why do many Oriental nations lag in the path of progress? Ignorant mothers, I dare affirm, is a most potent cause. The child will always bear the stamp of its mother. While the husbands are at their business during the day, the children are under the direct influence of their mother at home. Her every characteristic of conduct has a moulding influence upon the young child. If her words be wise and her conduct refined, the infant will thus be moulded; and, on the contrary, if she be ignorant and rude, she will reproduce her defects in her young child. Thus women invariably determine the standard of civilization of their country. It is altogether the exception for an empty-headed mother to raise up clear-headed, intellectual children. Mothers either bless or curse the community by their general standard. With woman's intellectual, ethical and spiritual elevation the nation rises, while with the degradation and humiliation of womanhood the nation sinks to the lowest level of civilization. If we traverse the ages covered by history, we shall find these statements fully verified. We need not go to past ages for conviction; compare the old stagnant dulness and darkness of some Asian countries of to-day with the bright and prosperous America, where her fair daughters share alike with man the highest education of the land.

Happily our Armenians are realizing this serious problem more and more in the education of woman. The social evolution of our people is to be counted for the female education which seems to be vitally connected with Christian faith, so largely accepted by our nation.

Is the Turkish woman responsible for the semi-civilized position she occupies in the world? As has been indicated, she is more than anxious to take her true place among her progressive sisters, but the religious institution under which she is unfortunately placed creates all these inhuman customs—seclusion, polygamy and blind submission to ill-treatment—which she is under moral bounds to obey. Her religious institution, therefore, is directly accountable for her sad position. Had Mohammed lived in the present era, I do not believe he would have approved these customs. The improvement or elevation of the condition of Turkish women, then, is to be only through a reformation of the Mohammedan religion.

While it is a great thing to know other people, it is a greater thing to know ourselves. A man does not know and see himself in a true and impartial light. His character, good or bad, is like a basket on his back. He may be conscious of it, but cannot see it as other people do. What is true of individuals is also true of nations.

Contact with various people on either side of the ocean has afforded me the opportunity to observe that of all nations the ladies of America are the most clever and bright; and they shine with splendor in social life. This is due, I venture to affirm, to the exalted position the women of this country enjoy above that of her sisters of other climes. As it has been my good fortune to see the extremes of contrast between female liberty and general conditions, I shall not hesitate to reflect my humble observations impartially and boldly as to the merits and demerits of either condition. Acknowledging the attainments of American ladies, their grace of culture, their exquisite manners and education, I disapprove of their unbounded freedom. Excessive use of even a good thing is a vice. It is a doctrine of Confucius that "true virtue consists in avoiding extremes."

As has been indicated, the Turkish woman is at one extreme of secluded privacy, while the American is at the other extreme of unlimited liberty. I condemn both extremes in advocating a balance, or the position of the Armenian woman, which in many respects I consider an ideal one. She enjoys the society of men to a limited extent. She does not hide her face from them, nor spare her modest words in conversation; yet she is not "gay" or "awfully jolly" in the company of men. She does not at the first acquaintance grow familiar with a stranger, nor use flippant and reckless words of double meaning. She does not dance in the arms of near acquaintances, nor walk and talk freely with them. Her words to a stranger are few and careful. Her favorite literature is not fiction, nor such sensational journals as are filled with crimes and infamy. She reads only such books as are of a clean and elevating character. The Armenian gentleman does not take

Armenian ladies to low theatres and similar places of amusement to jeopardize their innocence.

AN ARMENIAN LADY.

In a word, an Armenian lady is generally an ideal of purity, of loveliness of spirit and firmness of character. She is the queen of her home, loved and esteemed by her household. An Armenian young lady may have her preference, but she cannot marry anyone without the sanction of her parents. Is not this demand within the scope of common sense and of religion. She owes her life and existence to her parents, and should not her life's most important event— marriage—meet with their approval? If religion is considered, "Honor thy father and thy mother," was the commandment that God thundered from Mt. Sinai.

In many an American home broken-hearted parents are doomed to life-long unhappiness over the self-willed choice of their children. "Love hides a multitude of sins," but parents look beyond the boundaries of love. This Armenian custom of marriage, demanding the voice of the parents, is generally followed with happy results. There are no divorce courts among our people, no prostitute women, no ill-famed houses nor illegitimate births. Is it truly civilized this Western idea of granting the "fair sex" unlimited freedom, or is it really liberty for a helpless woman, who by such customs, becomes an easy victim to man, when she finds herself ruined and debased? When the finer elements of womanhood are transformed to the aspect of a hideous spectre; when she is cast out from the love and esteem of society, thus finding no refuge but the grave where she may bury herself with her shame. Watch the many tragic and heartrending scenes as the result of female freedom—too much freedom. Vice and crime are running riot in all the cities of the American Republic, which are unknown in lands where woman's liberty is somewhat modified. Truly, I do not believe in woman becoming the slave of man, neither do I believe in her becoming his victim.

Would suffrage really benefit womankind? Her dearest sphere has ever been the home circle, where she reigns supreme, educating her children in both morals and religion. Here woman has her rights unquestioned, and here her work tends to make voters for "God, and home, and native land." America has exalted her daughters, can she exalt their morals? America has granted freedom to the fair sex; can she not devise reformation for fallen women?

It must not be supposed that the vicious tendencies here noticed apply to American women as a rule, but that they belong to a class which these conditions of freedom, or the abuse of it, have made possible. Whatever may be said in favor of the opposite tendencies, as they apply to American women in general, we intend only to refer to a feature of social life, which, though exceptional, deserves the observations made, and calls more loudly for restrictive measures than for the enlargement of "woman's sphere."

Let us now look at some of the peculiar yet interesting customs leading to marriage. The matches and courtships with the Turks are beset with more difficulties than in western countries. Young Turks do not call on their lady friends and prolong the tale—indeed a tale of long hours among some Americans. Most Turkish girls cannot even write, but many generations of practice has developed an unique system of symbols by which they communicate with young men whose friendship they wish to encourage. A hanum or young lady sees in the private grounds of a neighbor over the wall, a comely youth whom she admires, and then proceeds to communicate with him. She prepares an affectionate surprise, not with paper and ink, for she can not write. She makes up an expressive token of regard with a piece of string, delicious fruit, fragrant flowers, and pretty bits of stone, each of which has a meaning. When completed it is tossed over the intervening wall, and lying near his favorite ramble is soon found. It is read like an open book. The thoughts expressed are those in vogue the world over under similar impulses, and ere long she will find an answer beneath her window similar to her own message. This strange correspondence will continue for a varying period. By and by, if the tokens are indicative of unalterable affection, the young man brings the question of his matrimonial scheme to the consideration of his parents, inspiring them with the same zeal and determination that Patrick Henry displayed in the Continental Congress when he exclaimed "Give me liberty or give me death." The marriage of the young lovers is arranged by mutual agreement of the families. This is but the formal sequel to an affair of the heart, romantic in its inception and natural in its results. With such a system of communicating her thoughts many a Mohammedan girl does not regret her inability to write. She has no conception of any other use which she could make of the pen. Doubtless she has been quite willing to submit to those forms of marriage ceremony and wedding festivity which make her the almost hideous dummy of the occasion. To be enveloped and thickly covered in a colored sheet and stood in the corner for hours, mute and motionless, like the corpse at an Irish wake, is the fate of the Turkish bride. She is not allowed to be exposed to the public gaze. It has always been a mystery to me how such an odd custom was ever inaugurated and still dominates for so many generations!—how life's most happy occasion should be spent in such a state of humiliation. Has not the Orient always been a land of mysterious operations? What a striking contrast to the free and happy lot of Armenian and other Christian brides at the hymenial celebration. Among the more old-fashioned parents, contracts for the marriage of their children are made while they are yet mere infants, and neither the boy nor the girl has any voice in the matter. The wedding festivities among the Turks last several days. It is made a great occasion of joy and jubilee, enlivened by music and dancing. The newly married bride's manners are very singular indeed, and in this one aspect bears a remarkable resemblance to the old-fashioned patriarchal manners of the Armenians. She utters never a word, except when alone with her husband. Nor will she until after the birth of her first born. Then she will talk only as young mothers can to her own. After awhile she will talk to her mother-in-law; still later, her own mother may again hear her voice, and ere long she will talk in whispers with the young girls of the household. She will not leave the house during the first year of her married life except to go to devotions. Practically her discipline as a bride terminates in six years; however, she will never in her lifetime open her lips to a man except he is related to her. Such exacting devotion is unknown elsewhere. Young girls of the household are allowed to conduct themselves in striking contrast to the young married woman. They chatter cheerfully while playing with white kittens, whose tails are dyed pink, in imitation of the Sultan's favorite horse. Their ruddy faces, full of mirth, are the brightest part of the domestic picture.

Among the Armenians the parents of the bride and groom send out a large number of wedding invitations to their respective friends and relatives. Thus the wedding becomes a picturesque concourse of guests, gathered from far and near, at the respective homes of the bride and groom, all dressed in gala attire, with profuse gifts on hand for the bride. It is, indeed, made the greatest occasion of joy and merriment. Everything puts on a most brilliant appearance. There is much gaud and glitter, pomp and pride all around. What a wave of rich robes! What a luminous vision of flashing jewels! After much music, hilarity and refreshments, the companions of the groom advance in procession to the home of the bride, and thence in great ceremony the joined guests accompanied by the bride and groom, proceed to church where the simple marriage ceremony is performed in the presence of many witnesses. In the evening there is generally a banquet tendered by the newly married pair to their happy friends. All next day, sometimes the entire week, the young couple are busy with congratulations of callers and feasting merriment. To make the greatest occasion in life—marriage, the greatest occasion of jubilee is certainly a beautiful custom, and Americans do well to adopt it.

THE CARE OF THE SICK—DISPOSAL OF THE DEAD.

After wandering together in the realms of fancy, courtship and marriage, I now invite you, my reader, to the city of the dead. Do not pleasure and grief, life and death, walk side by side through all earthly avenues? Are not our hearts sometimes enraptured with sunshine of joy, sometimes overshadowed with the thickest clouds of sorrow? Do not the objects in nature indicate the same law of life and death, of brightness and gloom? The exquisite flower that blooms to-day, holding in its sweet chalice the purest dews of the skies, fades away to-morrow. Shall we not, then, my reader, turn our steps for awhile from these brilliant nuptial pictures to solemn scenes of sickness and death.

In cities, medical science and treatment of the sick are very much on the same plan and condition as those among Americans. Within the last quarter of a century expert foreign and native doctors have multiplied in the country. In small villages and hamlets inhabited by Turks, the care of the sick is very singular indeed. Professional nursing is unknown, while quacks are numerous. The invalid wants to be cured at once—in a few hours. This universal desire to get rid of disease in a hurry makes them willing to try anything and everything that promises immediate victory over their malady. The larger and more repulsive the dose, the better they think their chances of recovery. They can not understand what good a few drops or a sugar-coated pill can do. They do not apply for a doctor until the sick is about to give up the ghost; in fact, the practice of medicine is not generally recognized as a distinct profession among ignorant villagers, but whoever has travelled and seen much of the world is supposed to know best what should be done in case of sickness. All intellectual foreigners, therefore, are considered to be doctors, and are constantly importuned day and night to treat their sick. Quacks, however, have their hands full. They give, for instance, the dust of the earth, plain white paper which would be soaked in water and administered in teaspoonful doses, or colored water to be applied in various forms, all of which pleads with mute eloquence for the medical missionary to save the bodies as well as the souls of those who have yet to learn that God's natural laws are as imperative as the moral code. Physicians have found that the natural vigorous constitutions of the people respond readily to scientific treatment when the quacks can be kept away.

All the relatives and friends of the sick are gathered around the bed of the sufferer, where they keep up a loud conversation, smoking their long pipes, laughing loudly, thus trying to divert the mind of the sufferer, while in a corner of the room the young boys play, spout and fight By such soothing processes the patient is sometimes lulled to slumber, often the slumber of death! No wonder the grave-yards are numerous and thickly populated.

Diseases vary, as elsewhere, according to locality and the occupations of the people. Smallpox makes sad ravages among the people at times, causing great loss of life. Pasteur's system of inoculation by virus has long been understood and practised here. Mothers are known to protect their infants from the virus of serpents and scorpions by giving them the diluted poison in infancy. Such children can be seen handling scorpions with impunity. Thus it would seem that Asia Minor was the cradle of modern applied science, as well as of the human race.

When death knocks at any door, that house is the scene of the wildest demonstrations of grief. Frequently the stillness of the night is so disturbed by the zealous mourners that sleep in the neighborhood is almost impossible. They cry aloud bewailing their loss. Sometimes they tear their hair, embrace the lifeless body, proclaiming his virtues if he had any; if not, then they create them. The burial follows with swift rapidity upon death. Soon the body is taken out into the yard, washed, wrapped tidily, placed in an open bier which is carried upon the shoulders of friends and neighbors, first to a church where the service for the dead is chanted, then to the cemetery, where it is placed in a shallow grave. The cemetery is often one huge common grave. Mohammedans, however, do not bury twice in the same place, which makes their cemeteries much larger than those of Christians. Among them, immediately after death, the body is removed to the porch of the mosque. After the usual noon-day worship, the congregation comes out to the yard of the mosque, standing up line by line in a silent and pious manner. As the holy man's powerful voice comes from the sacred schrine, the entire congregation take off their shoes, throw them on the ground and stand erect, putting their hands to their ears. At the second call all the hats are removed, and all heads are bowed down to the ground in rapt devotion; at the third call, the entire congregation, wearing their shoes and fezes, follow the corpse to the cemetery, where it is taken from the coffin and buried without any further ceremony. Then the coffin is taken back to the mosque to await another victim. Every nationality and creed have their own cemeteries at a distance from human habitations.

Individual graves of the Armenians have interesting monuments. Designs indicating the occupation or profession of him who reposes beneath are carved upon them. Those who suffered matyrdom have the fact indicated with a cross. A blacksmith's grave is, for instance, designated with the insignia of his calling.

In the Armenian provinces of Asia Minor, the oldest gravestones are very striking, from the fact that they are in the form of crouching rams, the inscriptions being cut on the sides of these elaborate monuments.

Mohammedan memorials are free from the desecrations too commonly seen in Christian cities of the dead. The headstone is a large monolith with inscriptions. At the foot of the grave is another of almost equal size. The space between is built up with marble slabs to resemble a chest or casket.

In large cities sepulchral forests of cypress trees make a profound impression upon the mind, as the coniferous tree casts its deepening shadows of mourning over the lonely grave. In his description of these cemeteries, how graphic are the words of Byron when he speaks of

> "——the place of a thousand tombs
> That shine beneath, while dark above
> The sad but living cypress glooms
> And withers not, though branch and leaf
> Are stamp'd with an eternal grief,
> Like early unrequitted love."

IN THE RURAL DISTRICT.

If you have leisure and fondness for rustic beauty, let us, in the bracing freshness of the air, mount on horse-back or on little donkeys, so numerous in the country, for outings. Let us seek a village and step within the threshold of a real old-fashioned Turkish house. On our way to the rural districts, as we pass joyously through leafy and flowery glories of the summer, giving and returning the salutations of peace and welcome, we should find much that is excellent and interesting both in objects and scenery. How our ears delight in the gentle rippling of the water intersecting our path, or the strains of the birds as we pass under the arching trees! How our eyes are greeted with lovely hillsides and dales, embellished by fragrant beds of wild flowers or by a vast

A CARAVAN.

camels of pure Syrian stock, journeying for many weary saats.* In the absence of railroads, these animals perform

---

*Natives reckon distances by hours and never by miles. Camels move at a rate of twenty-five or thirty miles a day with burden of nine hundred or one thousand pounds.

the duties of locomotives, although at a somewhat slower rate. The peculiar feature about this mighty host of camels is that they are led on by a little, sleepy donkey. This gives

A FREIGHT CARAVAN.

origin to one of our sayings, that when a mighty intellect follows the counsel of an insignificant one, they say, "the camel is following the donkey." Here and there we met

large droves of horses, buffaloes, sheep* and oxen, on the
great sweeps of grass. Yonder from the high wooded hills
a host of donkeys with loads of wood on their backs and
with loud jingling bells suspended from their necks, braying,
kicking and jumping, are marching to their respective
homes. Each donkey knows the house to which he belongs,
and needs no direction in finding the place. These little
creatures are collected from various houses every morning
by a donkey-man, and are returned in the evening with a
burden of wood for the use of the household. At our approach
to the cottage, all the dogs in the village are thoroughly
roused by our knocking. Our host is an ideal of a Turkish
patriarch, with a venerable beard on his brown, weather-
beaten countenance, sweeping down his chest. By common
consent he bears the title, *Coaja-Pashi* or "headman," of
the village. Like his fellow villagers, he is simple-minded,
good-hearted, honest, but unprogressive, an unambitious
and ignorant old man. He cannot read or write. He
knows no other literature and history but that of his
own immediate ancestors, and passionately cherishes
the legends and traditions of his fathers. He never
strives to keep up appearances. He wears a pair of
balloon-like trousers, of very voluminous folds. His
abba, or coat, is a long furred cloak of sheepskin,
with the woolly side turned in, in which he is constantly

---
*The sheep here, unlike those in America, have broad heavy tails of pure
fat, from three to six inches in diameter and about thirteen or fifteen inches
in length. In fact, the tail is one-half as heavy as the body of the sheep.
The fat of the tail is fried and used as lard in culinary operations.

enveloped summer and winter. His head is wrapped with a huge turban as large as a pumpkin. Like all neighboring peasants, his life is simple and his wants few. Many generations have wrought but little or no change in his modes and manners. He scorns all modern improvements, and watches them with much suspicion and prejudice. His bigotry and ignorance render him an easy victim to superstition, so any western farming machinery or advanced movement of any sort that might be beyond his comprehension, he pronounces "devilish" and has nothing to do with.

Rev. Dr. Cyrus Hamlin, ex-president of Robert college, says the Turks ascribe mechanical invention to Satan, the "stoned devil," against whom they pray five times a day. "I have myself," he says, "for some supposed mechanical ability, been seriously introduced by one Ottoman to another as 'the most Satanic man in the empire.'" Our Turk admits no innovation, as he never pretends or attempts any scheme which was not thought of and followed by his father; thus life flows on in the old channels. He is the head of a great family, grouped together on the mountain-side, by the sweeps of high, green meadows, and lives with his flocks and children—so many of them! An ample roof shelters nearly three-score members of the family, four generations under a single paternal roof, without knowledge or care for the world outside their little village. The glories of great cities, the pashas, and the pomp of royal dignitaries, are to them like a distant tradition. Yet they are comfortable, happy and contented in their little round of duties and pleasures, and are blessed with an easy-going temperament. The young man rises up with the sun in the morning, and

THE FLOCK.

with his flocks wanders over green mountains and hills, and shady groves and still waters, singing joyfully his native ballads through the woods, or playing his sweet-toned flute; returning home late, as the waning moon feebly lights up the exquisite landscapes. He joins the family dance by the blaze of their nocturnal fires, while the old women weave in cotton and yarn, or are occupied in manufacturing various articles for domestic use.

The house is built in a picturesque locality, by the old *Codja-Bashi* himself, who is the architect, the carpenter, as well as the government agent of the village. Logs are brought down from the near forest. The bricks are made with the intermixture of mud and straw, and are moulded in various sizes and shapes, then put in open fields to dry. Thus in a few days they become quite solid enough for building a substantial house for our old Turk. The earth which is dug out is banked against the sides of the house. The rear of the structure is entirely embedded in the hillside. Light enters through the oiled paper windows in the flat roof, or, when windows are discarded altogether, the occupants are content with what light penetrates down the low chimney, which is not higher than the roof—indeed, a peculiar home for a peculiar people. In the summer the stork builds her nest and raises her brood on the broad-topped chimney, quite undisturbed. In the darkness of night, the humble abode is illuminated by a feeble, flickering jet or olive oil wick. A brazier of charcoal-made fire is placed in the centre of the room, glowing almost as unextinguishable as the vestal virgins. It serves a double purpose, as a heater and over which the food is cooked. There are no tables, no books, no ornamental decorations nor chairs, but here and there are spread divans and *minders*, or cushions, with drapery of Kurdish stuffs, over which the occupants stretch themselves in cross-legged carelessness.

One or perhaps two large rooms are all in all for them, where they sit, sleep, cook and eat. The *Codja-Bashi*, with such crude belongings, never seems to think anything is lacking. On the wall, if we charitably term it so, or, rather on a partial partition, are saddles, bridles, guns, the entire paraphernalia of the field and chase, filling in the space between a sort of fence that separates the living apartments from the vast stable. The equine favorites are nearest the family. Like all Orientals and some Occidentals, the horse ranks highest in esteem as a domestic animal. Farther on are donkeys, wallowing buffaloes, cows and sheep, with chickens scattered between them.

As we step in the house we are received with a profusion of *salaams*. We at once find ourselves surrounded by a large Turkish family—grandfathers, fathers, uncles, brothers, cousins and numerous children, all thronged in the large room—dressed in gay and odd colors, sitting cross-legged around the bright blazing fire, and warming their lazy bones. But we fail to see in the great gathering any women, except the old grandmother, the senior wife of the *Codja-Bashi*, who is curiously dressed, or rather enveloped in a woolen garment from head to foot, and sits in a dark corner. The young Turks here must surely have some wives. In such a large family, doubtless, there must be some young girls, too. But where are they? All out of sight. As their religion does not allow women to appear in the presence of men, no matter how intimately acquainted, they are all driven into seclusion—a very bad custom, indeed! The more religious a Moslem, the more rigid the privacy of woman is enforced, and as a rule the country people in this neighborhood are the most zealous of religious fanatics.

I sometimes think if one of these over-pious Mohammedan Turks, by chance, should be dropped into an American city, and should see the young sons and daughters of Uncle Sam walking arm in arm in the full swing of social liberties, he would be shocked to death.

At the side opposite the darkest chimney corner, where the grandmother is, sits the *Codja-Bashi*, stretching his feet forth and smoking his long pipe, which is so extremely long that it extends from the corner to the centre of the room. In the course of our conversation the old man remarked concerning his residence, that his great, great, great (that great, however, goes about half a mile), father was born and died on the same spot where he now lives; and that he is about seventy-five years of age, but never has been a dozen *saats*, or hours, journey from his home. This is the case with many a Turkish peasant—many, indeed, who never set foot outside their farms. Our talk is interrupted, however, by the lusty shouting and fighting of the young boys. Then our host is obliged to go out among them with his ineffectual cries of anger and practical lectures. Before his return to us, however, he is called to another part of the house to quell a still louder tumult—ten or fifteen dogs are having a lively concert of howling and barking, so our good old *Codja-Bashi* is now on duty to establish peace among the dogs. On his return, let us ask him why he doesn't kill those useless brutes and get rid of them once for all? He will answer: "It is a great sin against Allah (God), and a violation of our laws." So numerous are the dogs, especially in the country, that when a Turk was once asked the population of his village, he answered: "About one thousand and sixty dogs and nine hundred people."

When the dinner time comes, all the males of the house return from the field, cleanly wash their hands and faces, and sit cross-legged on the floor in a circle around the sufra or low table. There are no knives, forks or plates. The bread is baked on the hearth on hot stones. In the centre is placed a common bowl of hot soup. So large was the bowl that I was about getting ready for a plunge bath, but owing to the fact that I was not a good swimmer, I feared that I might get drowned. When ready for the fray, the *Codja-Bashi* gave them the signal to commence. Immediately all the spoons enter the same unfortunate bowl. The soup was followed with a dish meat. Each rolled up their long, flowing sleeves, and with bare fingers and unbounded appetites separated the flesh from the bones, laying the latter on the platter. Then came the unfailing accompaniment, *yoghurt*, or coagulated buttermilk, a highly prized species of refreshment. After a succession of dishes, the ceremony of eating was ended with washing hands.

Codja-Bashi is the greatest scientific authority in the neighborhood. The fact that he is the oldest dignitary of the village, naturally makes him the authority on everything. One night the conversation of the family was interrupted by a bright flash of lightning, accompanied by heavy thunder. One of the children of the household thereupon asked the "grandfather" the cause of the bright light and the great noise; then the wise old patriarch grasped his sweeping beard and in a dignified tone gave this explanation.

"Up in the clouds," said he, "our prophet Mohammed and Christ went into business together, the profits to be divided equally. One night when Christ was deep asleep, Mohammed stole all the profits and left the place. In the morning Christ discovered the treachery of Mohammed, pursued him in his golden chariot, and so the noise of the pursuer and the rumble of the chariots is what makes the thunder. The lightning is the bullets of fire which Christ shot at his treacherous partner. At length poor Mohammed, finding escape in mid air impossible, suddenly plunged into a deep body of great waters, where he was quickly followed by Christ, and the terrible force of their conflict caused the waters to splash and pour down upon the earth, thus causing the rain."

This certainly beats all modern investigation. Alas! this is all his scientific knowledge. It is impossible to pound philosophical ideas into the empty heads of the Turkish villagers, because all intellectual studies are based upon traditions, which follow from generation to generation, and each "remarkable" son inherits the traditional knowledge of his great-great-grandfather. The odd part of it all is, that he is absolutely sure of the accuracy and truthfulness of his would-be knowledge, thus failing utterly to discriminate between reality and fiction, fact and fancy. The very idea of the word science does not seem to have entered into his empty head. To talk to these men of science is like talking to a blind man of colors.

The primary step to any sort of attainment is the sense and self-consciousness of ignorance. Do you want salvation? First find out that you are lost. Do you desire knowledge? First realize that you are ignorant, and thus come to the logical conclusion that you do need knowledge. Any individual who does not know that he does not know, shall never know any more than the nothing he does know. How sad to see in such an age of enlightenment midnight darkness settled down upon so many people!

Now let us watch how *Codja-Bashi* works in the field. He has no set time to commence his harvest; he takes his time, as there is not much fear of rain during the harvest season. As soon as the stalk of the crops are yellow or sufficiently matured, they are cut by hand with scythes and are piled up in the open field like American stacks.

In due season the piles are removed from various quarters near the village to the threshing floor, by large **arabahs**, or carts, drawn by buffaloes and heifers. The threshing floor is a hard and smooth circular piece of ground from fifty to eighty-five feet in diameter, upon which the stalk is strewn. Then the threshing machine, a mere sled, is driven around and around on the hard earthen floor by oxen, with a woman or boy standing on the sled. This threshing implement is made up of a hard piece of wood, and set on the under side with sharp flinty stones, similar to those of Indian arrow-heads. It grinds the straw into fine chaff and sifts out the grain. At the evening breeze, the threshed grain is thrown into the air with a light shovel. Thus the broken straw is blown on one side, leaving the grain of wheat on the ground for granaries. The chaff is also gathered and stored away for the purpose of feeding the cattle during the winter. This is certainly a slow and wasteful system of threshing.

The peasantry are poor and are kept poor, possessed of little more than what the craving of nature requires. Most of them, having no cash, pay their debts in natural products. The farmer's son toils and moils on the farm and does not migrate to towns in search of better employment, but stays where he is born—by his father's cattle. Thus they are immovable in their peasant instincts, as well as in their beliefs, ideas and usages. They are all devoted worshipers of the "almighty dollar," but are far from getting it, because they do not know how. They complain of the government over-taxation. Their dull and unenterprising character, I dare affirm, is a more potent cause of their poverty.

In such rural districts the old patriarchal administrative system is still in vogue, where within the crude and primitive log-house, by the hearth, sits the venerable *Codja-Bashi*, whose every word is law to all within. He is, as indicated, the agent for his community in all transactions with the government. In consideration of important affairs of general interest, he meets with the elders of neighboring hamlets, and, acting as a committee, they form the commune—a most striking illustration of the essential democracy of Oriental society, with the patriarchal system intact.

In high regard for family rights, it is superior to the Greek democracy. Under a fostering, dominant power, no reason can be given why it should not continue to the end of time as it has continued from the beginning. In times of adversity, it is a bulwark against anarchy and confusion. This system is a perpetual monument to the divine blessing on those who hold sacred God's first human institution, the family; indeed, all law originates in the family relation, the first institution for humanity established of God. All attempts to supplant it by military despotism, communism or celibate asceticism have been failures. The patriarchal system was the application of the family idea to the tribal relation. Recognition was the essential independence of tribes subject to treaty obligations, and the payment of taxes is the key to the permanence of Oriental institutions. This system, freed from man's abuses, has never been improved upon, and never will be.

As a supplanter and disturber of domestic felicity, it

brings its own punishment. On such a foundation a superstructure, though defective, may rest, and has rested securely for centuries. The defects of details are modified to some extent in our day by international treaties. May the chaff be removed from the wheat on the threshing floor of modern enlightenment.

Modern police courts of the Oriental capital are more like those of Paris than the old-time courts of the Cadis. The latter, like back-woods justices of America, substituted their own ideas of justice for established law. They would render justice against the defendant and send him to jail for not paying promptly, and send the plaintiff there too for making a fuss about so small a matter, while the witness would get a few days behind the bars for not minding his own business.

Numerous instances of just such cases of perverted judgment are on record. Fortunately, important matters must be referred to higher courts, where intelligence of becoming order holds the scales. The judicial system is so simple that the intelligent and conscientious administration of justice is not difficult.

The responsibility of religious and educational matters belongs to each nationality independently—Armenian Greeks and other nations adjust trifling disputes among themselves. Thus it would seem that the simple practice of justice to all would give an almost ideal government, at least in rural districts.

THE TURKS.

"Asia Minor is the recruiting-ground of the Turk, and is still almost untouched by the invader."—*Stanley Lane-Poole.*

THE early history of the Turks, if the accounts which we have of them can indeed be called history, is a commingling of war, romance of wandering conquests and glory of eastern court. For the poet, here are themes strong and untried. For the romancer, there is no dearth of fact as rich as fancy. The political economist here finds his theories in the frame-work of the material, and the historian in his portion, contrary to the common parlance, comes last and least. The name and race at its birth is in the swaddlings of mystery and myth. Near the central part of Asia twenty-two centuries ago, we find an empire spasmodically nomadic, composed of several kindred tribes, indiscriminately known by the general term Turks, they being of the same origin with those nomadic tribes, the Mongols, Tartars, Calmucks and Kirgis. The Chinese, dwelling some distance to the eastward, designated them by the name Hiongnu, or more literally Tu-kiu.

Whether or no the modern "Turk" is a corruption of the Chinese appellation, we are unable to say. We do know, however, from evidences that exist even at the present day, that this people, warlike and aggressive, overran Asia, even venturing so far north as the Lena and as far west as the Black Sea. The Chinese, who had long before held them in subjection, proved troublesome neighbors, and for three centuries constant war was waged between the two powers. The natural outcome of this was that the nation was split into a northern and southern empire. Among the rich mountains of the Altai were the lands of the northern tribes. They were not destined to remain there long, for the Southern Turks, uniting with their former enemies, compelled them to move westward. This was the first migration. These southern people in turn were forced by the Mongols and Tungusians to disperse.

The second great movement is known as the second westward immigration, and its off-shoots may be still found in both Asia and Europe.

It is the case with all movements truly great that the people who were destined to bear sway over the European Empire of to-day were humble in their beginnings. Looking back over the centuries, a little time after the two migrations mentioned, we find among the golden mountains of Altai a people, slaves to the great Khan of the Geougen. This slavery, in the light of later events, must be considered not a misfortune but a blessing, for it proved a most excellent school for the future conquest. Slavery is only a part of the history of the race, but ignorance is its condition. By employing these Turkish people in the manufacturing of arms, the masters were achieving their own downfall, for the former became so skillful in their use that they soon severed their bonds and established an empire under their spirited leader, Bertezema.

Much more than the allotted limits of this book would be required to portray in its true glory the grandeur of this earthly empire. We will simply state that this was an age of luxury and barbaric splendor, golden in fact and in figure.

It has been claimed by Turkish historians that their career as a people dazzles the mind of the reader, like gazing at the sun. The critical observer of history, however, will find in the weak and demoralized social and political condition of Asia Minor and the Byzantine provinces of Europe, a more potent cause of the success of Turkish arms than in the bravery and discipline of the Turks themselves.

From the accounts of that early period, in which legend and history are mingled, we can obtain but a faint conception of their early condition and manners.

It is obvious, however, that they had no fixed habitation, but, as it has been indicated, preferred a nomadic life in valleys and mountains, hunting and warlike exercises being their cherished occupations. This wandering life was so strongly developed into a national character, that even to-day we find the Turks chiefly engaged in pastoral and agricultural pursuits, while their neighbors, the Armenians, are largely devoted to commerce. Their tact and shrewdness in business have rightly won them the proverbial reputation, "It takes two Jews to cheat a Greek, and two Greeks to cheat an Armenian."

The early home of the Turks, Turkistan or Central Asia, was known among the Persians as Turan—the "country of darkness," and the inhabitants as Turanian "sons," or "people of darkness." Their religion, prior to Mohammedanism, was made up of their ancestral traditions and the doctrines of Zoroaster; they had their priests and worshiped fire, earth and water. The laws and regulations were communicated to the masses by the chiefs of the tribes.

The Seljukians were the first Turkish tribe to gain a place in history. They emigrated to Khorassan under the leadership of Seljuk, from whom they take their name. Here, in a Persian province, they founded an independent sovereignty. The able princes, Togral Beg, Alp Arslan and Malek Shah, extended the empire. Nowhere in Asia was such a succession of able leaders ever known. This heroic age of the Seljukian Turks corresponds with the Norman age in England; Persia, Armenia, Syria, the greater part of Asia Minor, and the region from the Oxus to the Jaxartes were conquered by them. Their greatest prosperity was under Malek Shah; agriculture was fostered, public works, such as canals, constructed. Learning was patronized. Their astronomers approximated closely the accuracy of the Gregorian calendar in reckoning time. In religious zeal they were the most intolerant of all Turks, and provoked the crusades. Upon the death of Malek Shah, his realm was divided into several small kingdoms, which made easy the advance of the Mongul hordes under Genghis Khan. This invasion resulted in the founding of the Ottoman dynasty. First these Seljukians, then the Ottomans, have ruled western Asia to this day.

We now come to notice the propagation of a force that was to have much to do in moulding the destiny of more than one nation. The religion of Mohammed, coming out from the Arabian deserts about the middle of the seventh century, spread with lightning rapidity through the zeal of his followers, north, south, east and west, until many tribes of Turks converted from Zoroastrianism and kindred religions, accepted the Mussulman faith. This occurred about the tenth century, although some historians claim the date much earlier. In following the fortunes of the people we are considering, it will be well to notice the influence of this great movement upon their national ideas and policy. One of its immediate effects was that instead of becoming peaceful, as might have been expected, the Turks coupled zeal for conquest with religious fanaticism. We find that at the end of the tenth century dynasties of Turkish princes in Palestine, Syria and Egypt, a sultan, Mahmoud by name, a powerful ruler, reigned in Eastern Persia and later as far as Hindoostan. Neither Mahmoud nor his son, however, enjoyed peaceful reigns, for in the regions of Bokhara dwelt a kindred race of warlike disposition, with whom the Sultan quarreled.

The political career of the Ottoman Turks commences in the thirteenth century, when a band of 50,000, driven out from central Asia by the Mongols, under the hereditary leadership of Suleyman Shah, penetrated *via* Persia into our country, Armenia. The sanguinary quarrel gave prestige to the present line of sovereigns of the Turkish empire in western Asia, and serves as the connecting link between the legendary and verified history of this notable Turanian family.

The next chief, Er-Toghrul, while advancing upon the frontiers of the Seljukians of Roum, aided Ala-ud-Din, the Seljukide Sultan, in his war against the Mongols. At the end of a successful contest, Er-Toghrul was rewarded by the grateful Sultan with vast lands of Byzantine provinces as the future home of his people. Er-Toghrul was yet alive when his son Osman, the founder of the present dynasty, comes forth in the annals of Turkish history in fanciful vision, surrounded with miraculous revelations and marvelous circumstances of birth. The sword of Osman is still worn by sovereigns at their coronation, and from him the native surname Osman and the European corruption Ottoman have been derived. Modern Turks prefer and take pride in the terms Osmanli and Ottoman, while the name "Turk" they consider a disparagement and insult.

During the famous administration of Osman, his followers spread themselves on the Byzantine frontier,

THE TURKS.

occupying the cities of Eski-Shehr and Karaja-Hisar. In his various wars, many possessions of the eastern Roman Empire passed into his growing states.

TURKISH FOOT SOLDIERS.

About the year 1300, the Seljukian Empire was destroyed by Mongol invaders. From the ruins, however, arose ten principalities, which, one by one, in due time, were joined to the Osman kingdom. Osman coined money and caused public prayers to be read in his own name (1301). These are the two essential prerogatives of an eastern sovereign. That date is practically taken as the birth of the Ottoman empire. He introduced the absolute ownership of land among his people. After a firm establishment of his power, he waged war against his old adversaries, the Mongol hordes, and drove them out of Kara-Hissar. It is alleged he was of such a just and generous character that the subjects of the eastern Roman emperor fled to his protection. It is commonly said that this wise and good Osman ruled after his death. His younger son, Orkhan, came forth with such unusual attainments of imperial wisdom and tact that he far surpassed his father's achievements. He became a master of a considerable portion of Asia Minor, as the mutual jealousies of the provinces of the empire made them easy victims to conquest. His reign marked the creation of a most vital military organization, that of the standing army. This new system came a century before the reign of Charles VII. of France, who is considered by the European historians of middle ages the originator of that policy.

His celebrated guards were known by the name *Yeni-Cheri*, "new troops." Corps of Spahis, or regular cavalry, were also organized. He married the daughter of the Emperor Cantacuzenus. As a potent advocate of science, art and religion, he promoted the cause of public instruction, endowing the state with various educational and religious institutions, and was greatly esteemed by men of learning who were admitted to his councils. His capital, Brusa, was made a centre of light. Considering the age in which he lived, he should be placed among the most illustrious of Turkish sovereigns, as a competent leader, prompt executive and wise legislator.

His son, Suleyman, co-operated in his father's enterprises, and was the first to embrace the idea of a European invasion. He planted the crescent across the Hellespont. The sudden termination of his life hastened the death of his broken-hearted father (1359). The second son of Orchan, Amurath, or Murad, inherited the crown and the military genius of his father. He strengthened his military corps, the Janizaries, by recruiting it from youthful Christian captives, who were thus dedicated to the service of the court and army. Their number and power was greatly augmented under succeeding sovereigns. He accomplished his burning desire to extend his possessions across the Hellespont into Europe. In 1365 he captured and made his European capital, Adrianople, then a most flourishing city of the Byzantine empire, rich in population and favorably situated at the confluence of three rivers.

This move was of momentous importance in furthering his designs upon Europe. The tidings of Turkish devastation so greatly frightened the Christians that Pope Urban V. pronounced a crusade against "the unbelieving Turks." In this the Kral of Servia, the Voivodes of Bosnia and Wallachia, joined with King Louis of Hungary in an expedition against Adrianople to drive the Turks back to Asian deserts. The Turks, however, under the cover of night, with shouts of Allah! Allah! inflicted

SULTAN AMURATH I. (MURAD.)

an overwhelming defeat on the united forces of Christendom.

Roumelia and Bulgaria were conquered and passed to the swelling possessions of the Sultan. His last famous contest against the combined forces of Servia, Hungary, Bosnia, Wallachia and Albania, was of an extremely desperate nature, in which the Sultan gained victory with the sacrifice of his life.

Bayezid the *Yildirim*, or "Thunderbolt," the son of Amurath, rightly earned his title, as speedy movements characterized all his expeditions. He extended his conquests east and west. He besieged Constantinople for years, and the emperor was compelled to recognize his authority in paying an annual tribute. While Bayezid was engaged in the East, the King of Hungary, taking advantage of his absence, with a large army of European knights, besieged Nicopolis. The "Thunderbolt," however, arrived at his lightning speed and overwhelmed the besiegers. Mongol-Tartars, under the leadership of wild Tamerlane, after causing serious destruction in Armenia, had penetrated into the Ottoman Empire. Near Angora, two determined hosts stood face to face. As the result of the furious battle Bayezid met his fate, his country was conquered and he was carried into captivity, where he died. Then the Tartars withdrew. A civil war of ten years ensued between the four jealous sons of the late Sultan.

Mohammed, however, succeeded in ascending the throne. He did not engage in annexation of new territories, but endeavored to be at peace and on amicable terms with the sovereigns of Europe. He was much esteemed by his subjects and the Byzantines. He had, however, a constant struggle with civil outbreaks. His death was sudden, at the early age of 33 years (1420).

It is needless herein to follow the administration of successive sultans. The sword of Osman descended in regular line of succession through many generations in the grasp of conquering sultans. Their brightest victory was the capture of Constantinople, the capital of the Byzantine empire. Its subjection was delayed by Tamerlane, the Napoleon of Asia, until the reign of Mohammed II, who overthrew it in 1453. The empire was extended eastward in Asia Minor and westward in Europe. There were internal revolts against the absolute power of the sultans, but they were always suppressed. Sometimes the Janizaries, the pretorian guard of the sultan, would depose him and put his son on the throne. An attempt was made to conquer Italy, but it failed completely. At this time a navy was maintained, which was the terror of the Mediterranean Sea. Early in the sixteenth century, by the conquest of Egypt, the sultan was able to negotiate with Caliph, who reigned a purely spiritual prince at Cairo, to make over to him the rights and privileges of the successors to the Prophet, at the same time securing the sacred banner and other relics of the founder of Islam.

Syria and the Island of Rhodes was conquered about this time. Soon after, the planting of the red flag before the walls of Venice by Suleyman I. marked the western limit of the Ottoman advance, for they did not take the city. Farther into Europe the Crescent never found its way.

Suleyman's reign was the high-water mark of Ottoman power. He had contemplated the subjection of the entire Occident, and was rightly surnamed the "Magnificent." From this zenith of glory, in 1526, the empire began to decline. Here followed a succession of weak and irresolute sultans. In the latter part of this century, an allied fleet, under Don John of Austria, dealt a withering blow to the Ottoman navy. A succession of wars followed with Austria, Russia and Poland. Success and defeat were about equally divided on the field. Gradually the vitality of the nation was drained by continual carnage. Austria no longer lived in continual dread of Turkish invasion, but took the offensive. European Turkey began to shrink in extent.

Egypt is only nominally a part of the Turkish Empire. Military insubination and revolts, troubles and hostilities of the neighboring districts, assumed more and more alarming proportions. Now and then courageous and wise rulers arose and somewhat brightened the political horizon, but under incompetent sovereigns, the Turkish nation relapsed into a condition from bad to worse. The present Sultan is a staunch patron of learning, who has endowed the state with schools for the education of his people.

The nomadic instinct of the Turanian family has not yet been extinguished in Asia Minor. Circassians, Tartars and Kurds and other cognate tribes, are to be looked upon as unmitigated rogues and thieves, whose only occupation has been kidnapping, plundering and destroying life and property. They want everything for nothing.

They visit the peaceful villages with fire and sword, extorting money and goods to gratify their lazy and luxurious tastes. With no feeling of mercy, they delight in blood and wasteful destruction. No language can depict

A KURD.

their atrocious cruelties and inhuman crimes. The above engraving, taken from a photograph, well depicts the characteristically hideous face of a Kurd. Russians, in order to relieve their minds from the gloom and terror of the Circassians, expelled them from their mountain homes of Caucasus. They, however, entered Turkey with gun and pistol, and without any restriction on the part of the authorities. Ever since they have become the scourge

A CIRCASSIAN

and dread of the surrounding country. They are admirable horsemen and marksmen. The above engraving is a faithful representation of a Circassian with his characteristic dress, with daggers rattling in his belt, and rows of cartridge holders ranged across his breast.

TAXATION IN TURKEY,

"Render therefore unto Cæsar the things which are Cæsar's."—Jesus Christ.

A RELIABLE index to the prosperity of any country is to be found in its system of taxation. Whether or no such taxes are proportionately divided, whether the poor are oppressed and the rich escape from their rightful share in the public burden of expense, are questions the answers to which, to a large extent, determine the character of the nation. The proper administration and regulation of public taxation has been a serious and unsolved problem in all ages. A wise administration of taxes has raised empires to the pinnacle of world-wide glory. A too-sweeping tax adjudication has led many a nation to irretrievable downfall. Taxation is the tyrant's mightiest tool; rightly conducted, it serves as the people's greatest blessing. One thing is certain, no matter how different the ways in which taxes are levied, they are essential to national growth and even national existence. In examining briefly the systems applied in Turkey to-day, let our judgment be deliberate, and let us ever take into consideration Turkey's own peculiar exigencies and surroundings.

Before proceeding to discuss taxation proper, a few preliminary statements regarding the currency of the country will be both necessary and convenient. The best known coin and the standard of currency is the official gold piastre, equal to four cents in United States currency. For convenience this coin is divided into forty paras, although a quarter-piastre, consisting of ten paras, is the smallest denomination in use. A para is about equal to one mill.

Beside the official, there are also two other inferior piastres, one of alloyed silver and copper and another of mere copper. There are two other denominations that might be mentioned: The lira, composed of one hundred gold piastres, and the purse of five hundred piastres, worth about twenty dollars.

Every year, at harvest time, a person called the *Multeyim* appears among the agriculturists and claims his one-tenth of the produce, such as corn, tobacco, cotton, grapes and wheat. This tax-collector has bought his authority from the government at auction, and the tax which he gathers in produce is the most ancient, and perhaps the most remunerative, and is called the asher, or tithes. The collector, as a rule, combines self-interest with public service in regulating the amount of contribution.

Although not always of the same proportion as at present, this tax has been levied from the earliest history of the country. At one time it assumed as low a proportion of one-fortieth, at another time it rose as high as fifteen per cent. of the produce.

Concerning this tax there is much complaint made, but we believe that the complaint is largely unwarranted, for the other assessments, such as are levied on property, are generally light. One good feature, which aids in doing away with corruption, is the fact that officers of the State are never allowed to bid for tithes. One of the evils arises from the fact that the poor farmer bears the heaviest burden. Again, it is often the case that the produce, after having been harvested, is held by the farmer who is often compelled to wait some time for the assessor, and whose stock is thus liable to spoil.

Taking all these things into consideration, we need not wonder that the average producer is inclined to cheat when such a thing is possible. If it were practical, it would better the condition of things much were the government to collect this tax directly. She herself would be the gainer and the agriculturist would surely be encouraged.

Corresponding somewhat to the *ashr*, or tithe, on arable land is what is termed the *sayme*, a tax on sheep, goats, and sometimes cattle. Before 1858, this was collected in kind, but since that time a money valuation has been placed and one-tenth assessed by the government.

Similar to the property tax in this country is the *Verghi*, which to-day assumes two forms, a tax on income and a tax on property. This is systematic, and based upon a fixed principle. The assessing of the income tax is conducted in a very fair manner, being levied in public meetings, at which all concerned are permitted to be present. The assessment differs with the professions and trades, and depends also on the reputed wealth of the individual. In general, however, it is three per cent. on all gross profit accumulations of invested capital or from any other source. There are a few who are exempt, such as parish doctors, religious orders and school-masters.

The tax on real property mentioned above is estimated at 4 per 1000 a year on the estimated or simple value of all lands and houses, whether subject to tithes or not. The value of such property is calculated at five times its produce or twenty times its assumed rent, and even with the tithe this should not be considered oppressive. It may be said that in addition, those who receive rent from tenants are required to hand over four per cent. per annum, tithe-paying land alone excepted.

Although in the year 1856 a decree was issued which admitted Christians into the Ottoman army, the law has never been fully enforced, owing to several important obstacles. Above a couple of regiments of mixed Cossacks, there are hardly any non-Mussulmen engaged in the service. The exemptions from military duty, however, is not to be obtained for nothing, and a tax commonly termed the *Bedel*, is laid upon all non-Mohammedans not in the army. Although much complaint is raised by Christians against this tax, it cannot be said to be very unfair, considering that a

Mohammedan has to pay more for the exemption than does the Christian. This tax is also levied in different forms, according to the province and the attendant circumstances. As with the others, the greatest evil of this assessment is that it seems to fall almost wholly upon the poor, who, unlike other subjects, bear the burden without striving to elude it.

This chapter being written for the general reader only, there is no need of going into minute details regarding the customs duties of the Turkish empire. Tables concerning the annual imports and exports are to be found in a number of available volumes.

Some reforms have been instituted of late years, which have greatly enhanced the prosperity of the nation. For instance, the eight per cent. tax, formerly imposed upon goods passing from one Turkish port to another, has happily been abolished and an excise of one per cent. placed in its stead.

The policy that places an eight per cent. tariff on all imports, indiscriminately, is not one that can receive the sanction of political economy. It is one that is open to no little abuse, the tariff being so manipulated that favoritism is frequently shown certain parties. The tax on exports is placed in the same uniform manner, at one per cent.

Various attempts have been made to develop the rich natural resources of the empire and establish manufactories, especially in the country, labor being so abundant and cheap. At one time a new era seemed to dawn, and thousands of natives were employed in factories. English and French influence, however, inaugurated the policy of free trade. Their goods were imported at a tariff of six or eight per cent. ad valorem. As a natural consequence, the Turkish factories were closed. Workingmen and their families were reduced to abject poverty.

The famous Bruse towels were imitated and sold much cheaper, driving out the native goods, which, though costing more, would last five times as long. Combs, cutlery and silks came from Sheffield, Manchester and Lyons. The fine silky fleece of the Angora goat is sold cheaper to the English manufacturer than to the native artisan, and comes back enhanced in value from fifty to one hundred fold. It is safe to say that of the wealth produced by a native goat, forty-nine dollars out of every fifty goes into the pockets of foreigners. America may well learn a lesson from the Angora goat, and keep on bucking and kicking against the free-trade system that has closed the factories, destroyed the revenues and produced beggary in the Ottoman empire.

The Turkish government has, in the last half century, run somewhat in debt, and its direct borrowings form no little portion of the general budget. The revenue was, in 1889, $90,000,000, while the expenditures were about $125,000,000. The national debt of the Turkish government is more than $500,000,000. It cannot be disputed that Turkey's system of taxation has its good as well as its more unfavorable side, and yet reform would do wonders in some quarters. We have no doubt that in time these reforms will come. Agriculture of different kinds would receive a valuable stimulus were more money expended for roads and other facilities for transportation, and the government would receive much more from taxes on such produce were she to conform to the sentiment of many of the nation's best citizens and collect her revenue herself directly.

MOHAMMEDANISM.

"There is no God but God, and Mohammed is his prophet."—*The Mohammedan Catechism.*

TO present herewith a historical account of the rise and progress of Mohammedanism is unnecessary, as that knowledge may be acquired in a number of creditable volumes; yet a brief description of their present religious state, traditions, customs and practices, from personal observation, we hope will prove interesting. The Koran, the work of Mohammed, and the holy book of the Islam world, contains many passages of high morality and also of common sense, and in instances almost joins hands with Christianity. This is due to the conformation of a number of the Old and New Testament books into the existing traditions of the people, the two elements being curiously intermixed to form the visionary ideals of the new religious creed founded by Mohammed, who took Moses and Christ as masters in law and ethics. A translation from the third sura of the Koran will best illustrate and confirm this assertion.

"When the angel said, 'O Mary, verily God sendeth

thee good tidings, that thou shalt bear the word proceeding from Himself. His name shall be Christ Jesus, the Son of Mary, honorable in this world and in the world to come, and one of those who approach near the presence of God. And He (Jesus) shall speak unto men in His cradle and when he is grown; and he shall be one of the righteous.' She answered, 'Lord how shall I have a son since a man hath not touched me?' The angel said 'Lo, God createth that which he pleaseth.' When he decreeth a thing, He only saith unto it 'be,' and it is. God shall teach him the Scriptures and wisdom, and the law and the gospel, and shall appoint him his apostle to the children of Israel. And He (Jesus) shall say, 'Verily I come unto you with a sign from your Lord, for I will make before you of clay as it were, the figure of a bird; then I will breath thereon and it shall become a bird by the permission of God; and I will heal him that hath been blind from his birth, and the leper; and I will raise the dead.' But when Jesus perceived their unbelief he said: 'Who will be my helpers toward God?' and the apostles answered, 'We will be the helpers of God; we believe in God, and do thou be as witnesses that we are true believers.'"

Christianity and Mohammedanism have more in common than any other two religions. Both proclaim the unity and fatherhood of God and the brotherhood of man. There is "no God but God," declares Mohammed. Christ is considered as one of the six apostles of God, and His Virgin Mother, one of the four perfect women. The following passage from the religious code of the Moslem, chanted in the Mosques, bears a certain resemblance to our Apostles' Creed:

"Allah is sole and eternal. He lives and is all-powerful. He knows and sees everything, is endowed with volition and action. In him is neither form nor figure, nor bounds nor limits, nor numbers nor parts, nor multiplications nor divisions; because he is neither body nor matter. He has neither beginning nor end, but exists by himself, without generation, without an abode, independent of the empire of Time; as incomparable in his nature as in his attributes, which, without being separated from his essence, do not constitute it."

Yet with these conformities, there are some points of contest and contrast between the two religions. Christ came to earth as the prophet of the spiritual life, declaring that his kingdom was not of this world, while Mohammed comes sword in hand. The religion of Christ is the law of love, proclaiming the great work of atonement The religion of Mohammed denies the Divine act of redemption, substituting an abstract Monotheism. As has been indicated, though Islam believes like Christendom in the fundamental idea of the unity of God, she rejects the doctrine of the Trinity. Again, the Koran furnishes both the code of law and of morals, thus the religion of the desert, and the political codes, inaugurated centuries ago for a wild and barbaric people, are even to-day appointed to govern the civil state and the morals of a people everywhere in contact with civilization. Thus the old civil laws of Mohammed, the worn out timbers, are still in use by the Moslem in building up their modern civilization; while, on the other hand, the Bible of the Christians furnishes only the moral code of its followers. Christ was not a politician. He did not enforce any civil or political dogmas. Even the wise Mosaic laws are deemed out of date, for as they were given to a particular people, in a particular country at a particular time, they are not to govern the nations of Christendom to-day.

Again, Christian ethics penetrate the inner life of man. They emphasize not dogmas or words, but feelings and acts, which alone make words valuable; not truth in the abstract, but goodness in the concrete. On the other hand, Islam utterly fails to discriminate between form and essence, substance and appearance.

Let us now look at some of the strange aspects, formalities and beliefs of this religious institution, and close our chapter with an impartial comparison of the two great religions.

Mohammedanism is essentially a religion of a form, hence the disciple of Islam does not thank God for past blessings, or implore his protection for the future, though he prays five times daily. Islamism means submission. Hence the efficacy of the service is in the number of times the *nemaz* or prayers are said. Before prayer a preparatory service of ablution with cold water is obligatory. If this is not done with strict conformity with the established usage, the subsequent prayers would be of no avail.

In the court yard of every mosque a large basin of water is provided, and the faithful standing straight and facing due north or south and advancing in order to it says "*Bissmillah*," meaning, it is in God's name I do this. The hands are washed to the wrist, the mouth and nose three times; then beginning at the toes, the feet are washed to the ankles, after which the right hand is dipped gently into water and a part of the head is wet. The arms are washed to the elbows, beginning at the finger tips. Then the rest of the head is wet, the water being dipped up by the right hand. The inside of the ears must also be washed with the index finger of either hand, and the back of the ears with the thumb. So extremely exacting is this ritual, that the slightest digression or omission necessitates the doing of all over again. Practice makes them expert, however, and they learn to do it quickly and correctly according to the requirements. The ceremony is repeated three times. Exemption is allowed where no water can be obtained, but the form must be gone through by touching the hands to dry earth or brick, instead of dipping it into water.

The time for prayers is regulated by the sun. Morning prayer is said between dawn and sunrise, and this makes the Mohammedans early risers. Noonday prayer, just as the sun is passing the meridian. An afternoon prayer at any time between four and five o'clock. The fourth prayer at sunset. The last prayer of the day is said before retiring.

The ritual for prayer is as rigid as that for ablution. It is not optional but imperative.

At almost every quarter of a mile are built the mosques—solid, substantial buildings. The minarets are the most beautiful spires that pierce the Levantine skies—symmetrical, lofty and majestic. They contain niether pealing chimes nor tolling bell, but five times daily from the top of these is heard the muezzin's *ezan* or call to prayer, in deep, long-drawn tones.

Allah Ekber! God is Almighty!

Ashadu inna la-ilaha il allah! I testify that there is no God but God!

Ashadu inna Mohammed dur resool ullah, sally-ullahu alayha va Alehe! I testify that Mohammed is the apostle of God; the blessing of God be upon him and his family!

Hyya alesselah! Hasten to prayers!

Hayya alelfelah! Hasten to prosperity!

Hayya ala khyr-ul-amel! Hasten to the best work!

Allah Ekber! God is Almighty!

La-il aha il allah! There is no God but God!

That voice is mingled with sacred cries from all the minarets of the different parts of the city—all Arabic—strange, yet heroic and impressive in tone. The voice resounds in the lightest pitch when he sings with three-fold iteration, *Laha il allah!* or "there is no God but God!" At this call all the faithful Moslem leave their engagements at once and hasten to worship, no matter how inclement the weather or how pressing their business engagements.

Their regular attendance and punctuality is bewildering to the Christian world. Would that our good Christians, who are required by the Divine Master to sanctify but one day in the week to devotions, would take lessons from the Mohammedan, and not rob the Lord of His own day by using it to their own pleasure and comfort. If any Mohammedan is late, he may at any time join with the congregation in the service, but the blessing to be obtained is far inferior to what would have resulted had he been on time. Tradition says a follower excused himself to the prophet on the ground that he was saving his friend from drowning, and hoped that he should be blessed for the kindly act as well as those who were early at prayer. The stern prophet would not accept the apology. "Though you had camels enough to fill the road from Mecca to Medina, all loaded with jewels, and should give the cargo to the poor, the blessing following would not equal those of promptness at prayer. Should you commit the whole Koran to memory and repeat it twice every night, the blessings received would not equal those of beginning *nemaz* (prayer) with the *Iman* (priest). Should you kill all the enemies of Islam, the great rewards would not compare with those of him who is prompt at the beginning of prayer. If by a word the heavens and earth could become paper, the sea be turned into ink, and all angels stand as scribes, yet they would be unable to write all the blessings you may enjoy for beginning prayers with the '*Iman*.'" The Mohammedans are deeply conscious to all these warnings of their prophet

Though not "in spirit and in truth," yet they worship according to their forms most faithfully.

The interior of the mosque is considered most holy, consequently all the people take off their shoes as they step within the shrine, and go through a series of pious movements. The religion of "the Prophet" forbids pictures, images or any other representation of the human form in their houses of worship. On the walls, however, are many inscriptions from the Koran. Censors burning olive oil are suspended by lines from the dome.

The floor is beautified with the richest rugs in the Orient, upon which Moslems prostrate themselves in their devotions; each follows the movement of the *Emir* (priest), raising the hands and bowing simultaneously with almost military precision.

While at prayer certain acts must be refrained from, as any of them would destroy the efficacy of the devotions. The full list is long, but in part it is: Looking around; striking a fly to kill; raising a foot from the floor; scratching more than three times in one place on the body; laughing loud enough to be heard.

The Iman who performs the devotional ceremonies preaches no sermon. Every day at noon he reads two chapters from the Koran, and then descends to mingle with the many worshipers, placing himself on a level with the common people.

On Friday, the holy day of the Mohammedans, the ceremonies are conducted with unusual pomp and ceremony, the

Koran being read before prayers are said, and on feast days both before and after prayers.

MOSLEM AT PRAYER.

The language of the Mohammedans in Asia Minor is Turkish, but the Koran is written in classical Arabic, an unintelligible tongue to the masses and only understood by a few of the best educated. Though the Koran is not intelligible to the masses, their tradition teaches that the mere hearing of the sacred book read has a miraculous effect in benefiting the soul and body, and so they are made content with the mere sound of meaningless words.

The reward of the faithful after death, as promised by the Koran, is all that could be desired. The prayers that he has said will light up his grave as a lamp. No sin will remain to be imputed to him at the resurrection. Angel wings will bear him aloft. Even should some sin remain through careless praying, he still has a chance of escape, though he does not believe in purgatory. If he has children, their innocence will admit them, and their grief at leaving their father behind will take him through the gates, Peter or no Peter!

Once in Paradise the Mohammedan has but to express his wants and they are immediately granted. His food is served on a golden plate, and the bones of the bird that has been devoured will again assume full plumage and fly away to sing as of yore in the leafy bowers. Wine, which is denied to the faithful here, will be abundant there, but will not intoxicate. The humblest in rank will have seventy-two virgins of immortal youth and angelic beauty to attend him. In eternity, momentary pleasures of time are to be extended to a thousand year. In brief, an ideal temporal paradise, based on the sensual pleasures of earth and taste, is to be magnified a thousand-fold beyond the utmost limit of even an Oriental imagination to depict. Such is their elysium.

If the rewards of fidelity are ideal according to sensual standards of pleasure, the punishments of the lost are cruel to the other extreme. The graves of this class are beds of hot coals, where the bones are piled one on another for want of room, and fused at white heat without loss of the sense of feeling. Thirst and hunger, with scourgings, will add the spice of variety to this roasting scene, until the resurrection, when Satan will assume exclusive control and do as he likes with them for ever more.

Here a brief description of Mohammed's utopian journey to paradise would fittingly illustrate some of the singular aspects and ideas of Mohammedanism.

The angel Gabriel appeared to Mohammed with an Alborak, a strange animal—a cross between an ass and a mule. This long eared brute began to talk, demanding some concessions from the new prophet. Having promised the creature a golden stall in heaven, Mohammed was permitted to mount. In the twinkling of an eye he arrived at Jerusalem, where, after a pleasant interview with the patriarchs and prophets of all ages, he ascended, with Gabriel, a ladder from the "city of David" to the "city of God."

As he arrived at the portals of heaven, he saw a large inscription on one side, "There is no God but God," and on the other, "Mohammed is His Apostle."

The heavenly host being informed that Mohammed had come, at once the pearly gates were thrown wide open, where entering, he was quickly embraced by great old Adam, who was happy to meet his most illustrious son. From this heaven the stars, which he described as being hollow, round silver balls, were suspended by golden chains. [What would become of faith in Mohammed's visions, if modern science were introduced among his followers!]

Quickly Mohammed was taken from the first to the second heaven—a journey of five hundred years. Here he met the angel of the cocks, who was so tall as to reach from the first to the second heaven. Nearly every morning this big rooster joins God in singing a song that fills the entire universe with its melodious strains. Every being on earth hears them but man. In this heaven he met Noah, the presiding dignitary. He was tendered a most cordial reception as he passed through the golden streets. In the third heaven he describes the angels as being very large; one of the most gigantic required 70,000 days' journey between the eyes. Here, too, he found the same inscription as in the first and second heaven. After a short interview with Moses in the fourth heaven, of emerald construction, he was taken to the fifth to meet Joseph; then to the sixth heaven of carbuncle, where he beheld John the Baptist.

Radiant with light and ruled over by Jesus, was the seventh heaven. He was attended by a vast multitude of joyous inhabitants. Innumerable angels of this heaven were of dazzling beauty. Each one of them possessed 70,000 heads, with 70,000 mouths to each head, and 70,000 tongues to each mouth—all singing and singing day and night everlasting. Here the prophet, with a glorious pomp, was presented to God, whose face was concealed by 70,000 veils. Here, too, on the sides of the divine throne, Mohammed beheld the inscription "There is no God but God," and on the other, "Mohammed is His apostle." God, after saluting Mohammed, commissioned him to return to earth with full authority.

Charity is prescribed by the Koran for the faithful in two forms—voluntary and compulsory. The latter amounts to the fortieth part of his possessions, but is only imposed when the property aggregates a certain sum. Voluntary charity is usually dispensed at the time of the feast following the annual fast.

The pilgrimage to Mecca is a pious duty. It is believed to bestow certain inestimable privileges to all who can possibly make the trip. Nothing could test faith more than that long and tiresome journey. All the world has heard of the vast concourse there annually assembled from all parts of Asia, Africa and Europe. At that time every highway leading to the sacred Kaaba, becomes a field hospital of the sick and dying. Physicians and nurses are generally wanting, however. When cholera prevails, as it usually does, Mecca becomes the disseminating point for the most fatal of diseases.

Honors are bestowed on the survivors of the hazardous ordeal of this journey, and they are addressed by the title, "Hadji." Among the Armenians, the same title is applied to those Christians who have visited Jerusalem.

These Christian "Hadjies" usually have a small cross

tatooed on the hand, to indicate the fact that they have made the pilgrimage to the Holy Sepulcher.

Mohammed has declared that he will not intercede in heaven for unmarried men. So marry you must, men, or take your chances. Remember Mohammed, old bachelors and old maids, miserable in this world, miserable in the world to come! The Prophet would have them bring up large families, that his followers may outnumber all others in paradise. The widows actually pray, "Let me be married before I die, that I may not be ashamed when I meet Allah!" Allah will reward the parents of children, those who pay the debts of another, and the soldiers in holy wars.

Like other religious institutions, Mohammedanism has its holidays, feast and fast days. The most important of these is *Orooj* an annual fast last twenty-nine or thirty days, or the entire month of *Ramazan*. The fast cannot begin until the new moon has been seen. In cloudy weather messengers are sent to the peaks of mountains, and there ascertain the appearance of the new moon. The Sultan telegraphs to all parts of the empire for the fast to begin. Local announcement is made by the firing of cannon at sunrise. During the daytime, for a month, Mohammedans abstain from eating, drinking, smoking, and some go so far as to talk very little, for fear they may take too much air into their mouths, and thus break their fast, in which case they would have to keep the sixty subsequent days.

Even the touch of a Christian is avoided during *Ramazan*. As every physical enjoyment is proscribed but sleep, devotees sleep nearly all day, except when at worship. "Blessed be the man who first invented sleep!" Those wandering in the street are like mad-men, so Christians had better keep out of their way. The asking of questions by "infidel dogs" is promptly rebuked. The law is paralyzed. The fact that they have all been fasting is a sufficient excuse for all sorts of wicked performances. Business is at a standstill. Fanaticism has full sway.

At home, on the day of *Ramazan*, toward evening, with food prepared, all await the signal cannon. At sunset minarets are illuminated, the cannon is fired, and at the muezzin's call from the slender spires, the fasting is suddenly changed into feasting. Night is virtually turned into day. There is a hasty scramble for something to eat, excessive eating, dancing, singing, continue until the latter part of the night. This fast and feast is held in honor of the time when Mohammed claimed that God revealed the Koran to him. Moslems believed that Abraham, Moses and Jesus also received divine revelations during this month.

There are many who attribute this celebration to another event. One day when Mohammed was wandering in the desert, one of his camels fled. Poor Mohammed pursued all day without eating or drinking, and captured it about sunset. Mohammedans are not certain which day of the month this occurred, so in order to make sure they celebrate the whole month.

The green turbaned Turks are the descendants of the Prophet Mohammed, through his daughter, Fatima, who

A DERVISH.

married Ali, the faithful disciple. They are known as *Emirs*, and enjoy religious and political preference. Having a chief of their own, who is a sovereign among them, even to the infliction of punishment, they form a religious institution, keeping alive the spirit of Islamism, as the Janizaries in their day kept up the military spirit of the empire.

Besides these there are several other peculiar Mohammedan orders. We shall first describe the Dervishes. The Dervish is a historic figure. The order was founded thirty-seven years after the death of Mohammed. Asceticism is the most distinctive feature of this order. On several occasions it has been my privilege to visit the huts of these sacred beggars. They are destitute of furniture. Some of the rigid devotees have not even a cushion or bedding, and lie on the bare mud-floor. As their maxim says, "poverty is my glory," they generally live in deserted quarters of the city, in mud holes or in mountain caves. Like the Grecian philosopher, Diogenes, all their care in life is a place to sleep and something to eat. In personal appearance they are the most hideous-looking beings on earth. They wear sheep-skin, have their whiskers and hair hang down long over their faces and shoulders. They always carry sharp hatchets in their hands for protection, and go begging in the bazaars, and praying in the streets in the Arabic tongue. Cut off from all family associations, their lives are entirely sanctified to their monastic institutions.

There is another kind of Dervishes—religious dancers, an entirely different order from those above described. In manner, dress and principles, these latter are more human, though at times quite frantic. These are spinners and howlers. The former are generally found in *tekiehs* or chapels—octagon-shaped rooms with polished floors. They are in close-fitting suits with loose petticoats, and wear conical hats of grey felt. After the Koran is expounded and kisses exchanged, the graceful spinning begins. Arms are crossed on the breast with hands on the shoulders. Slowly at first, then faster, as they warm up, the arms and skirts are extended. They move around and pass one another but never touch. Steadily the spell increases, until the climax is reached, when it decreases to the finish, about one hour being the time for a single dance.

The howlers are the demons of religious fanaticism. In a shell of a building, decorated with spikes, chains, daggers and like implements of torture, with which they excite themselves, arranged in circles, they repeat all the names of God. Swinging backward and forward, they cry "*La-il-la-il! La-lah! Hoo-yah Hou!*" Beads of perspiration form on the faces distorted as if by mental anguish. Foaming at the mouth like madmen, they proceed with the fearful energy of deep fervor and rapture of devotion, until, all the physical powers overcome by exhaustion, they fall bleeding to the floor. Calmly a devotee may approach the Sheikh and have a skewer thrust through his cheek. You may examine and see that there is no legerdemain.

There is still another class, which represents the climax of Mohammedan fanaticism. While in Constantinople in the summer of 1889, I was permitted one night to witness the horrid religious celebration of the Persian Mohammedans—an awful night, never to be forgotten! The purpose of the celebration is to obtain merit and forgiveness for admittance to Paradise without examination. It was during the month of *Ramazan*—a month of religious frenzy

DANCING DERVISHES.

and fanaticism in the calendar of Mohammedanism, that the Persian devotees, clothed in robes of white, appeared in a procession at night. They were all armed with swords, iron chains and like weapons of torture. The streets were surging with thousands of clamorous men and women of every nationality and type, who were in eager anticipation of the death-foreboding pageant soon to come. Then from a large building, amid a profusion of lamps, the Persian devotees burst out into the streets in the midst of the many spectators, and moved step by step in a circle, amid wild roars and wails of Hassan! Hussein! Hassan! Hossein-Shah.*

They inflict ferocious charges upon their bodies, some slashing themselves to slices or mutilating themselves by clubs and iron chains, many gashing their heads and throats with knives. It is the most horrible spectacle ever performed by a group of savage mortals, where the body loses all semblance of humanity and assumes the aspect of a hideous ghost. Hassan and Hussein, murdered twelve centuries ago, that night claimed the active sympathy of their followers with fresh blood.

Ears, eyes, hands, arms, head, throat and abdomen are not considered too dear to be sacrificed in this deamon-like act of religious frenzy. As the blood pours out in streams, sobbing cries of Hassan and Hussein go on in varying tones and inflame the entire assembly.

My very soul shuddered and recoiled with horror as

---

*Hassan and Hussein were sons of Fatima, and grandchildren to Mohammed. Their father, Ali, a favorite of the Prophet, became Caliph later in his order, and upon his assassination in 660, theirs was the right to the Caliphate. Hassan gave up his claim to prevent war, and was finally poisoned by the tyrant Yazid. Twenty years after his brother, Hussein, was slain in battle, just as he had been invited back by the subjects of the empire. The injustice done these two has always been the cause for comment among a certain class of Mohammedans.

I gazed upon faces bathed with the blood and sweat of this most extreme torture. Many more and more violently keep step with the wild performance until, their physical powers overcome by exhaustion, they lie gasping for breath, some never again to stagger to their feet. Some women, moved by the agony of the impotent rage and misery, fainted away. Who could look on such a scene unmoved?

Before this awful sight we close our eyes, and the hardest heart turns sick and faint. In an anguish of despair the soul cries out, O God, is Thy light powerless to penetrate the midnight that hangs pall-like over benighted people of Thy own creation? And peering through the darkness, hope sees the glimmer of a star, the morning star, bespeaking a larger light, before whose powerful rays this awful night of ignorance shall flee forever.

At this Mohammedan paroxysm of self torture, the oft-repeated question echoed to my ear with more emphasis than ever, "Why art thou a Christian?" and my soul answered, because God is love, His religion is a religion of love, a religion of peace. No more sacrifice, for Christ suffered all our transgressions, and we are free from all penalty. We are not required to commemorate His blood with our blood, but to follow the path of eternal life and happiness which he has opened for us through His death.

There is much misunderstanding among Christians and the world in general regarding the Mohammedan faith and worship. Especially among the Christians, ideas of Mohammedanism are inexcusably vague, and are consequently obstacles in the way of a correct understanding of the history of a religious force that has had no little part in the history of the world.

If the follower of Christ will study the Koran earnestly, he will not fail to find many features that strikingly resemble the leading texts of his own faith. Indeed, he will be surprised to find that the religion which he formerly supposed to be the offspring of heathenism, abounding in superstition and folly, is pregnant with truths that have been inculcated into his own heart and life since childhood.

And it is not difficult to discover a reason for the similarity. That Mohammedanism should resemble Christianity, and that the Koran should compare closely with the Bible, is only a natural outcome of the training of the great Prophet.

From his earliest years he was taught the Old and New Testaments, and rendered them a love and respect which he did not withdraw in his old age, for to the last he spoke of the Bible as the word of God.

Besides the direct influence of the Holy Scriptures, the surroundings of his household were essentially Christian in character. His favorite wife embraced the teachings of Christ, one of his other wives was a Jewess, and most of his highly esteemed counsellors were of the Christian persuasion. All this could not fail to exert a powerful influence, and Mohammet manifested it in all his writings, paying homage to Christ to the last, and looking upon him as the greatest of prophets.

The question naturally arises, "If this is true, why did Mohammed seek to establish a new religion?" If such was his inner loyalty to Christianity, why was he a traitor to his convictions?

Besides shedding a ray on our own understanding, we will be doing Mohammed justice if we class him among the reformers. He did not claim to be more than a man. Although his followers ascribe them to him, he did not pretend to perform miracles, and, in fact, went so far as to denounce them.

Had his work been accomplished in a more enlightened country, he would not have been falsely canonized as a prophet, but would probably be known as a Christian reformer. He fought not against the Bible, nor against Christianity in its purity. He did, however, zealously attack that Christianity as corruptly practiced by the people of his time. One of these corruptions, a very natural result of the metaphoreal character of certain scriptural passages, was the apparent apotheosis of Jesus and the Virgin Mary, the popular conception making the latter a goddess and the former a God, equal and separate from Jehovah. This was very obnoxious to Mohammed, who, like his followers of the present day, and the Jews of his own, believed in the absolute unity of the deity. The teaching of the Koran in this regard is almost identical with that of the Bible, and other points of resemblance, indeed of ideality, may be very easily designated.

For instance, the Koran teaches the existence of angels

as God's messengers. It is interesting to note, however, that where the Bible makes man a little lower than the angels, the Mohammedan supposes the heavenly host, in the glad morn of creation, kneeling and paying homage to man, God's last and most glorious achievement. Again, Mohammed taught that our lives are in God's hands and nothing can happen to his creatures save what He Himself has meted out of His all-wise providence. All things that happen belong in the course of a God-destiny. Fate was a word with which the great Prophet had no patience "Fate is not; our times, on the contrary, are in His hands."

With Christians, the Mohammedans hold the tenet of inspiration, believing that God has certain chosen men with whom he confides special messages to be transmitted to his people—a fact of marked import, as an indication of no little height of religious dignity. As if foreseeing, too, the discussions that would inevitably arise over the question of inspiration, Mohammed shrewdly divides inspiration into two classes—direct and indirect. In the one case the dicta of the deity are transmitted verbatim; in the other, the Prophet used his own forms of expression, but writes under the divine influence and direction. This is not unlike the most recent theories of Christian apologists in regard to Holy Writ.

With Christendom, again, the Musselman believes in rewards and punishments, in the resurrection, and in a day of judgment, when each will be judged according to his deeds in the flesh. And with no essential difference he believes in a heaven for all who have lived uprightly, where friend is to meet with friend and wife with husband (this latter somewhat contrary to Christian teachings). And here we would have something to say concerning those who find fault with the picture which Mohammed draws of the celestial paradise, censuring him for depicting it as a place of sensual joy and allurement. In the first place, this charge is practically groundless. In the second place, we would say that to our nation it makes no essential difference how we describe the land of the hereafter, so that we make that description conform to our ideas of true and pure happiness, as all conceptions employing the material as symbols of the spiritual must necessarily fall far short of the true glory of heaven. Whether we make it a city with walls of jasper and streets of gold, echoing to the ring of happy harps, or see with tranquil vision an infinite paradise, clothed with wonder and peopled with creations of eternal love, we achieve as much and as little. Neither is heaven; both are faulty metaphors, halting figures, imperfect symbols.

The memory of devastating wars waged by Mohammed; the atrocious cruelties perpetrated by his followers upon those of unlike faith; the fact that polygamy has existed, and apparently was sanctioned by the great Prophet himself—all conspire to breed an antipathy within us that is not wholly justifiable. We have already spoken of the near kinship that Mohammedanism bears to Christianity. The commands of the Koran in regard to methods of warfare, and its admonitions deprecating cruelty in any form, are as strict as those found in our own sacred scriptures. And in justice to all, it cannot be said that Christendom has been much more humane in her warfare in the past; so that, although the Mohammedans rightly merit condemnation, it is only another instance of trying to take the mote out of our brother's eye, while our own is in the same condition. As to polygamy, which is rightfully repulsive to every person of enlightenment, we would say that although Mohammed is reported to have had many wives, he did not teach the practice, except in cases like his own, when suffering and want could be alleviated by an introduction of worthy women into a good home and easy circumstances.

Polygamy, also, while perhaps an evil in itself, is a remedy for many evils, somewhat more dire, in society and state. A public woman, in the immoral sense of Christian Europe and America, does not exist in Mohammedan Turkey. Let him who is somewhat skeptical of the good influences of the Mohammedan religion draw a comparison between the sobriety of the devotees with the inebrity of America. No legal restraint is employed, but crimes arising from immoderate drinking are very few, and all owing to the strong spiritual influence of a religion that Christians rightfully pronounce a mistake, but wrongfully despise. We would be far from defending Mohammedanism in all its teachings and practices. There is much to be condemned, but let us not forget that there is much to be commended, and much that should tend to link us with our somewhat mistaken but sincere brothers. In all our judgments let us be liberal, and let us not forget that our God will not judge them guilty who with heart and soul worship Him in word and life, according to the measure of the divine light shed upon their yearning hopes and waiting souls.

THE QUEEN OF THE EAST.

" 'Tis a grand sight, from off the Giant's Grave,
To watch the progress of those rolling seas,
Between the Bosphorus as they lash and lave
Europe and Asia."—*Byron.*

" To see Rome and die is merely gratuitous suicide when the other Rome, the beautiful city of Constantine, remains to be visited."—*Lane Poole.*

MAN is an emotional being just as truly as he is a thinking being. He ever admires the beautiful; his imagination is alert to grasp fancy pictures in nature and in experience. Youth has youthful admirations, maturity loftier ones. "The Queen of the East" was the dream of my youth. In the school-room, its rich historical associations were studied with enchantment; at home, around the fireside, its many stirring incidents and daily social events were the subjects of our conversation and hours of reading. In my dreams its splendid palaces, its modern and ancient temples, rose before my imagination in all their grandeur. At last the happy day came, when on my way to the American shores I beheld this Mecca of my imagination, and spent some weeks amongst its mosques

and shrines. The voyage from Samson to Constantinople was my first experience with the sea; it was short but tiresome, and rendered still further unpleasant by constant seasickness. So utterly miserable was I, that I almost hoped at times that a fairer land might be my home before I should reach America. But in the brightness of a lovely morning, when we sailed into the calm and sweet waters of the Bosphorus, my illness disappeared or was quite forgotten in the scene before me. Oh! visions of brightness, inspiration of my youth! Here was the Constantinople of my dreams, no less fair than I had deemed her, sitting supreme on her seven hills, at the juncture of Europe and Asia with a foot firmly planted on each. My curious eyes, with those of many others who crowded the deck, were strained to catch glimpses of the villas and palaces stretching from the Black Sea to the Marmora, a distance of twenty miles, now approaching, then receding, as the historic strait, narrow when we enter it, widens into a broad expanse of clear waters, washing the slopes of blue-clad, olive-crowned hills, studded with the solid palatial homes of the rich and the nestling villas of the well-to-do.

As we pass, on the European shores are the diplomatic villages of Buyukdere and Therapia, and later Roumili Hissar claims our attention, with its formidable battery below, while in the distance Robert College can be seen outlined against a perfect sky.

On the Asian shore, Anadolu-Hissar fronts Roumili

Hissar. At this point Europe and Asia stand face to face at their nearest approach, and the magnificent palaces of Oriental and Occidental aristocrats cast a deep shadow upon the blue waters of the Bosphorus. As we advance on the southern side, "Golden Horn," a curved arm of the sea, stretches before us with miles of city.

Yonder, beyond the Seraglio Point, rises the swelling dome of St. Sophia, and a thread of mosques, with glittering minarets cleaving the blue of the sky that crown the successive heights of Stamboul. Opposite this Galatian splendor rises Pera, with the pomp and dignity of aristocracy, while a famous bridge connects these two points, upon which men of every color, type and language pass to and fro in a mighty throng, to the amazing interest of any spectator, who finds Orient and Occident, hat and fez, black and white, all mixed and mingled in a common tide of humanity, everything novel and strange!

After the setting of the sun, as I glided along the historic channel, under the canopy of heaven, admiring the exquisite colors of sunset die away beyond the rolling hills of the Asian shore, and watching the stars twinkle out from their infinite vaults over the calm waters of the Bosphorus, reflecting in their depths the flags of every nation that flutter in the breeze, which at this hour creeps from peak to peak along the shore, I was thrilled with the thought of the changes these waters had seen. The nocturnal stillness which is disturbed only by the wild roar of the far-away

waves, echoes to my listening ear with the thunder of conquerors, under whose mighty tramp those hills and mountains were shaken to their foundation. Here powerful kingdoms flourished and vanished. Oriental and Occidental civilizations collided and combined. The greatest religious minds of the world gathered here to solve the mysteries of religion. The song of poets and eloquence of orators blended here with the profound thought of philosophy. Constantinople! the great bone of contention of all nations, of all ages.

"Give me Constantinople and you may have the remainder of Europe," said Alexander of Russia, when he met Napoleon the Great, to discuss with him their mutual interests. "What!" answered Napoleon, with a very emphatic exclamation, "Give you Constantinople? Never! Why, that is the key to the whole situation." And as ancient Byzantium, it offered to the mind of Constantine an ideal military position, fit bulwark of Christianity against Asiatic fanaticism, and he accordingly made it the new capital of his empire in 330 A. D., giving it his own name.

As a radial point for commerce, too, it is unsurpassed. Here the artizan finds his skill in demand to supply the wants of all the nationalities of the world. In this mart the astute merchant finds a market for his wares from whatever clime they may be brought. Its avenues of trade radiate to all parts of industrial Europe. Northward it is the gateway to Russia, southward it includes all Africa in its commercial relations. Through the Suez canal is the easy route to India, and eastward are the pillars of Hercules—a living, breathing cosmos of the human race. Moreover, the city is to-day, as of ancient times, the ecclesiastical center of surrounding nations. This is the seat of the Armenian Patriarch, the Exarch of the Bulgarians, the Patriarch of the Greeks, the Azkabid of the Protestant Armenians, the Monsignore of the Catholics, Khahambashi or high priest of the Jews, and Sheick-u'ul Islam of the Mohammedans.

The climate is most salubrious and healthy, the skies of purest azure blue. The sunlight glare is lost in invisible vapors from the near approaching seas, which have given the city the ancient title of "The City of the Three Seas." Cooling zephyrs blow almost constantly over the city's hilly slopes and through her great watery highways.

Byron has said, "It is a delicious sight to see what Heaven hath done for the delicious land;" and the Greek colony that founded here ancient Byzantium, must have exclaimed in their hearts: "Here is indeed the earthly paradise, fit dwelling place for gods."

At sunrise, the vista to the eastward is delightful, the rosy glow of snow-clad Mysian Olympus making on the mind of the beholder an impression never to be forgotten. The waters which confront the observer at nearly every point by day, produce a sublime effect in the moonlight. The city is swathed about in a mantle of glistening whiteness. Her domes, palaces and minarets, refulgent in the silvery light, compel one to exclaim in rapture, "Bride of the Orient! would that as much had been done by thine inhabitants to make thee good and desirable as nature and art have done to make thee beautiful," for when we enter the city's heart, the poetry of the distant view is lost in the medley of men and animals contending for a foot-hold in the filthy streets which we tread. Numerous dogs are seen, and the fact that they are artful and cunning dodgers is understood by the way they prefer to collide with the legs of pedestrians, in preference to the heels of donkeys or the fore-feet of camels. In the hum and buzzing of the streets, scores of them will claim the right of way when contesting for a bone, and men afoot may find their best clothes where their feet should be in the mad rush of these useless brutes. The noisy jargon of many languages, the jostling of porters under heavy loads on backs, with the venders of ice-cream, sherbet, etc., all mingling with the donkeys, horses and "precious" dogs in the highway, makes a street scene unparalleled in the world. Are you weary of the street? Step into a cafe, always near at hand, and note the quiet comfort of Turkish luncheon at all hours of the day. Women are not seen here. The servants are neat and tidy. Viands served are clean and wholesome. Coffee is the first thing; smoking follows the meal. Here we have time to reflect on what we have seen as we came along. Mosques, tombs, and the ruins of former greatness in irregular succession. Of these, the tombs of the founders of mosques are the most beautiful and richly embellished, the railing within sometimes of solid silver. The mosques, too, are very magnificent. They are more than five hundred and fifty in number. Among them St. Sophia, the mosque of Sultan Achmed and that of Suleiman are the most elegant and imposing structures in the Sultan's empire, and deserve special mention. The latter, located on the Golden Horn, was modeled after St. Sophia. It has four minarets with three galleries. The interior of the shrine is commensurate with its external grandeur. The mosque of Sultan Achmed, erected in 1610, is the only one in the Turkish empire that has six minarets. On account of its convenient location in the Hippodrome, it has always been the scene of the Sultan's triumphal processions on annual festivals and other religious celebrations. Its interior is spacious and airy, but it is to St. Sophia that we must turn for the real, dazzling embodiment of Oriental magnificence.

While in Constantinople, I was anxious to visit this most historic shrine of St. Sophia, but I was warned that no native Christian visitor is allowed within its hallowed precincts. Upon hearing this caution, I was the more determined to enter. "Where there is a will there is a way." My companions and myself, uniformed in Turkish costume, speaking Turkish, with a grave look passed in. I never shall forget the effect wrought upon me by the sight of this sacred edifice. I was compelled to pause hours in a spell of mighty wonderment. I could almost see the Emperor Constantine in his last fervent supplications to God. I could almost see men, women and children as they rushed from the fire and sword without, into the holy

shrine, in the hope that the angel of God would protect them from the avenging blow of the conquering Turks. I could almost hear with the clang of arms, the heart-rending cries, the prayer, the sob, the vain appeal for mercy, when the doors of St. Sophia were broken with axes, and thousands upon thousands were slaughtered in warm blood. (These melancholy recollections sent a cold horror chilling through my veins). I could almost witness how the Christian cross, the saints, the images were put out, and the crescent and Mohammedan inscriptions were placed in their stead.

St. Sophia is one of the oldest monuments of Christianity. A thousand years older than St. Peter's at Rome, I found it cruciform, about three hundred by two hundred and fifty feet in dimensions, supported by two hundred pillars, surrounded by a dome one hundred and eighty-two feet high. It has a seating capacity of twenty-three thousand persons. It was rebuilt by Emperor Justinian, and opened on Christmas of the year 548. In its erection, which occupied seven years, were employed one hundred architects, one hundred master masons and ten thousand fellow craftsmen. On its completion, Justinian exclaimed : "I have vanquished thee, O Solomon!"

Where the Hippodrome once stood is now the At Meadan, an open square of the city, and there still may be seen a few of the art treasures that made ancient Byzantium famous. It is nine hundred by four hundred and fifty feet, built originally after the circus at Rome. The

SANTA SOPHIA.

conical column of three twisted serpents, on whose head once rested the tripod of the oracle at Delphi, is still there. There formerly stood four famous bronze horses of Lysippus, now ornamenting the forehead of St. Mark's church in Venice. Lonely, solemn and going to decay, stand the historic columns of Theodosius, ancient Cistern of Constantine, a subterranean chamber of six hundred pillars, the water from which supplied the army during sieges, and ruins of the aqueduct complete all that remains of ancient Byzantium.

The walls of the city, no longer a means of defence, are crumbling away. They extend along the water front, then overland about four miles to the Golden Horn. Once pierced by forty-three gates, but seventeen now remain. Outside the walls, a line of cypress groves mark the cities of the dead. Superstition causes the Turks to shun these places by night. Brave in war, they dare not challenge the ghosts of the grave-yard in the dark. So it happens that thieves and cut-throats have a safe and notorious place of resort just "over the wall," and on Friday, the Mohammedan Sabbath, the afternoon of which is given to recreation, these cool and quiet walks are thronged with the poor of the great city, seeking here the nearest approach possible to nature's shady solitudes, while the elite, both native and foreign, go up the Bosphorus to a point called the Sweet Waters of Europe—the Newport of the Orient. Thus these places of the departed afford a double asylum to the wretched and the oppressed.

The visit to the Sweet Waters of Europe is made in brilliant equipages or on horseback along the shores, or in georgeous boats and barges, which latter, owing to the extended water front of the city, are almost as much a feature of the place as are the gondolas at Venice. The scene is a bright one, for the Turks are given to finery and display, and the uniforms of all the navies of the world enliven the pageant.

Instead of resorting to these places of rest or amusement, the very pious, on Friday, visit mosques and tombs; and another gala feature of the day is the passage of the Sultan to prayer. Nothing in the ordinary routine of daily life in Constantinople interests the people more. Thousand upon thousands of citizens and strangers gather along the route of the imperial pageant. The procession is never postponed—at least one thing in Turkish affairs occurs on time.

The custom had a singular origin. In 1361, Sultan Murad I., having offered to give evidence in a court of justice, the judge refused to hear his testimony, because, according to the Koran, no one could be a witness who had not joined in common prayers in the mosque. The Sultan admitted the justice of the decision, and on the next Friday proceeded to the mosque in great state, to engage in prayers as one of the worshipers. The custom has been observed with religious regularity ever since. It gives the people an opportunity to see their ruler riding in state once a week. Even fatal illness does not deter him from going.

In two instances the Sultan has expired immediately on his return from prayers.

There is not the grandeur about it now that there was centuries ago, when the costumes were of velvet and gold. The highway through which he passed was then carpeted with richest Oriental rugs. Silver and gold coins were strewn in his path. The new mosque, in which the present Sultan worships, is but five minutes walk from the palace. He rides to it, however, in an elegant barouche, with all pomp of elaborate ritual and imposing ceremony. From the palace to the mosque, the streets are lined on either side, four ranks deep, with brightly uniformed regiments of gorgeous Oriental soldiers. It is carpeted a half inch deep with fine, clean sand. At the Imam's call, the Sultan "the light of the sun" and the "shadow of the universe," emerges from his seclusion, enters the gilded royal carriage and, preceded by the few veiled ladies of his household and young sons and male relatives, proceeds to the mosque. It is the most gorgeous royal event of frequent occurrence in all the world. The Caliph of the 200,000,000 Mohammedans in the world, and sovereign of the 85,000,000 of the Ottoman empire (1,200,000 in the city alone), appears amid the acclaims of the immense throng of people, attended not only by his own household, but by the brightly costumed ambassadors and consuls of all nations. Official horse-tails, which have led to victory or defeat on a thousand battlefields, jewel-hilted swords, sashes, turbans and fezes, worn by the males in line, even to the little boys on Arabian steeds, lend the charm of novelty to a pageant which for magnificence merely is seldom equalled under the sun. After a half hour at prayers, the return to the palace is made in similar order.

The present Sultan, Abdul Hamid II., though a young man of great intelligence, is delicate, with a pale face and weak figure. I had glimpses of him one Friday noon, when he was going in procession to the mosque to worship. He lives in palaces of dazzling beauty at Seraglio point, by the banks of the Bosphorus. He is the supreme head of the state, with absolute theocratic powers; that is, he is the Caliph or the pope of the Mohammedan world, as well as the unrestricted political power of his own empire. Of late years, however, his power of absolution has been somewhat modified by the interference of the European governments, and by the demand of the expounders of the Koran, that the Sultan should adhere strictly to the teachings of the holy book, which teaches no such doctrine.

Of the royal household, the following may be mentioned: The principal honorary officer of the court is the imperial sword bearer. As his duties are few, he is seldom called into the Sultan's presence. Those in most intimate communication with the Sultan are his private secretaries and chamberlains. As they enjoy the relation of intimate personal friends, their favor is eagerly sought by aspirants for political recognition. Then there are gentlemen of the household, who are trained from early youth for their respective duties. They begin as cup-bearers or gentlemen

IMPERIAL PALACE OF DOLMA-BAYTCHE, ON THE BOSPHORUS.

of the wardrobe; or they manipulate the slippers, pipe and delicate coffee cups. Their elegance of manner and intelligence is quite striking. From pages, they are promoted to be chamberlains or even ministers of the state.

Mutes are a very unique and indispensable part of the Sultan's household. When private interviews are held with the Minister of State, all others withdraw, but the mutes remain. Even when the Grand Council meets behind closed doors, they are present to wait on the high dignitaries. "Having ears they hear not," yet sometimes understand more than they pretend, and have been known to communicate important state secrets to their friends. In olden times they were the executioners, perhaps because they could not hear the heart-rending cries of the victims.

Dwarfs are kept as court-jesters. A Sultan wishing to test the ingenuity of his dwarf, called one into the harem and told him he might have his choice of the girls as his wife if he could kiss her first. The little man cast a longing glance into the face of a Circassian beauty as she towered above him, and instantly struck her smartly on the chest. The unexpected assault nearly doubled the young woman, when the dwarf, taking advantage of her stooping position, kissed her and won from the Sultan a handsome wife for his tact and audacity.

When calling on the Sultan, one meets at the threshold the gentlemen of the household. Passing these personages, one ascends a flight of stairs and finds himself in a large hall with curtained doorways leading to the various apart ments about it. This is the *selamlik*, "place of salutation." It corresponds to the American reception room. Before one of the curtained doorways the guards, or "curtain keepers to his majesty" are stationed. Their presence indicates where the Sultan of Sultans will be found. The accredited visitor entering this room finds the lineal descendant of Osman, seated on a wide Turkish sofa, with a desk before him, a graceful *chibouk* or Turkish pipe, with amber mouthpiece, studded with diamonds lying carelessly at his side. A word from the sovereign, attendants appear as if by magic, and stand in a row with folded hands before him.

No one is ever seated in the presence of the Sultan. On the presentation of an ambassador, the event is so contrived that the Sultan enters at one door at the moment that the diplomat enters at another. This is done that the distinguished guest may be received by the Sultan standing, without that dignitary condescending to rise.

Like all cities, particularly all old cities, Constantinople has its quarters. Near the Seraglio Point, so named from the palaces of the Sultan, which, as we have seen, are located there, is the landing place for vessels, and this is the quarter for the native shops or "bazaars." Here one must keep a sharp lookout both upon the quality of the article he would purchase and the price he shall pay. With the Musselman to get the best of the bargain has no possible moral significance, and is merely an intellectual feat. Unlike the foreign trader, he never solicits your patronage, but receives your approaches to trade with the quiet dignity of a superior doing a favor. The goods are for sale, however, and a shrewd Yankee may get a good bargain by being persistent in demanding cut rates. It will take him longer, however, to buy a scarf or shawl than it would take to transfer a house and lot at home.

THE BAZAAR.

An Oriental bazaar is a mart of luxury and expense, a vast shop of wonders—an eternity of curiosities which has always been a source of interest and entertainment to those who are strangers to eastern life. Here the babbling rills of life flow hither and thither. All antagonistic races, creeds and tongues, with every shade of complexion, in an infinite variety of costumes, are here mixed and mingled—not as we see them at international expositions, but in the full swing of real life. Semitic Jews are here, as they are everywhere, with their short stature and long attenuated countenances. Bronze-colored Arabs with keen coal-black eyes, in their flowing robes and loose trousers, singularly contrast with the Mongolian negroes with curly hair and black round faces. The Aryan group is represented by Armenians and many Europeans, with their well-bred, dignified carriage and uniformity of dress. Persians in their sheep-skin caps; keen-eyed Greeks, cadaverous and proud, with the steady, stalwart sons of Uncle Sam, complete the motley congregation, except, indeed, for its predominant element—the red faced, lofty Turk. The babel of languages, the rush and crush of carriages, dogs and busy people, do not affect his cool, calm disposition, or quicken his steps, for Mohammed has said "to hasten is devilish." So he walks under his turban, his head filled with a feeling of pride, that this great *pot-pouri* of commerce and scenic enchantment is in some tense his.

Every avenue of the bazaar is appropriated to a particular branch of commerce, called a bezaustein. There are, for instance, the shoe bazaar, the confectionery bazaar, the armory bazaar, where weapons of almost every period and nation are exposed for sale, each occupying a separate avenue or bezaustein. The avenue of money-changers and bankers, a trade almost entirely monopolized by Armenians, is a glittering scene, where jewels, torquoises, pearls, brilliants and the most costly gems in the world are in store. The embroidery and shawl bazaars present a most gay and novel appearance, where hang Broussa silks, Genoa velvets, European satins, hangings of Tyrian tapestry, shawls from the goats of Thibet, Koran-inscribed Damascus sabres and rich scarfs, from the costly looms of Persia and Mecca, vieing with each other in beauty of design and richness of color. These, of all the bazaars, have an air the most Oriental. Let us approach this one midway, where the stuffs seem particularly rich. Ah! the aristocratic tradesman has already a customer—an American, certainly, from the particularly frank and natural bearing, a westerner, I should say, from the attire—perhaps a Chicagoan. Here are the fifteenth and nineteenth centuries face to face. The

Oriental, who of all Orientals, has never emerged from the middle ages, the Occidental, who of all his brethren has his foot most firmly planted on the threshold of a new era. In the one to sell is a stilted, etiquetical ceremony, in the other to buy is a necessary act, to be performed with the same freedom and naturalness as eating or breathing.

"How much will you take for that shawl?"

"Does his lordship refer to this delicate Persian fabric?"

Often the sharks apply titles of distinction to American purchasers, knowing only too well how susceptible they are to this subtle form of flattery. If they ever "talk shops" at home, however, I have no doubt they confess it works best with the women.

"I mean that reddish buck-colored thing, here, this!" pulling it down rather unceremoniously.

"Your lordship will observe that it is very delicate."

"I don't think it will wear very well, but what do you ask for it?"

"It has lasted already more than a century. It is still fresh. The gentleman's great-grand-daughter should most certainly wear it."

"Not married, my good friend, it's for a sister you know. What's the price of it? Is it really a hundred years old?"

Again the wily Turk has touched a weak spot, for the newest of nations has proverbially the greatest fondness for old things.

"Oh! your lordship is from a new country. I have

carpets here that have been slept on by ten generations of noble blood. Will the gentleman look at this rug of Bokhara?"

"Not now," says the pertinacious Yankee, "How much is this shawl?"

The Oriental sees it will not answer to delay any longer naming a startling price, so he says indifferently, "$900.00 is a small sum, your lordship."

The Turkish trader guesses your nationality at a glance, and is always ready to deal with you in your own coin, and to talk in its figures. His friend, the money changer, will make that all right for you, and at a better rate of discount, too, than you will find anywhere in the city.

"$900.00!" exclaims the westerner; "you might as well say $9000.00.

Oriental dignity is offended at this. The turbaned Turk draws himself up proudly, and turns to arranging his other wares, saying quietly, "The gentleman may take the shawl. It is his—a free gift."

Then the Yankee tries his game, too. As if tired of dickering for the shawl, he picks up a Damacus blade lying beneath a pile of tumbled silks.

"What's this?"

"A blade of Damascus."

"Is it a good one?"

"Let his lordship bring the tip and the hilt together, so;

bend it farther if you choose, it will never break. Swords of the kind are not made to-day."

"This is old, too, I suppose."

"The Sultan's signature, which you will find on the hilt, is that of the great Sultan Aladin, with whom the English fought for the tomb of the prophet Jesus."

"But if it bends so easily, you couldn't kill a man with it."

"The gentleman may try."

"On myself?" laughing.

"On his humble servant."

These extravagant remarks of the Turks are not jests, but the mere forms of politeness, and expected to be taken seriously.

"What are these marks engraved on the blade?"

"Verses from the Koran, promising rewards to those who die in battle, fighting for *Allah*.

Then, under his breath, and making a slight salute: "There is no God but God, and Mohammed is his prophet."

The westerner is by this time convinced that his deflection from the main point is to no avail, the Turk will go on forever about the Damascus blade, apparently quite oblivious of the fact that there had been any talk of buying a Persian shawl. If the buyer wants the shawl, he must come back to it himself.

He does so in his own characteristically abrupt way.

"Well, how much have I got to pay for this shawl?"

"His lordship is a gentleman. He evidently wants the shawl greatly, I will part with my treasure for $800.00."

"I will give you $300.00."

"The gentleman is jesting; some Persian woman toiled twenty years perhaps to complete this wonderful fabric. Such articles are the work of a lifetime."

The American has taken out his money. He counts out $300.00 and says nothing. His lordship wouldn't have me the loser on his account. It is eight years now I have kept this shawl in my shop, waiting for a purchaser wealthy enough and worthy to carry it away. I must have $700.00."

"We are wasting time, my friend," says the foreigner, who seems somewhat experienced, "you know you will sell this article much less than that, so why not name your price?"

"Camels brought the delicate fabric over many miles of desert—a long and weary journey. I have given the shawl to the gentleman, but he would not accept it. I think he can easily give me $550.00 for it."

"I am a good ways from home, and if I get rid of all my money, how shall I get back?" uneasily, but his countenance does not change its expression nor his manners descend to haste.

"By the beard of the prophet, it has cost me more. I must be in need of bread before I could part with so rare an article for such a price. I can show you many shawls for that figure, but I could not sell this one for less than $500.00.

From this point on the abatement of price is by smaller and smaller sums, until it goes down a dollar at a time.

"His lordship is indeed in a strange land. The prophet bid us be kind to strangers. I would sell it to the gentleman for $475.00."

"My friend, I have told you how much I will give. You see it here. I cannot give more."

He holds the money under the glittering black eyes of the trader. He, too, knows his antagonist's weak point. The glistening coin is a temptation. The Oriental's fingers work. Suffice it to say the Turk will move steadily downward on his figures, but at his own gait. He cannot be hurried by importunity or indifference, by argument or by direct appeal. Moreover, he will never come quite to his antagonist's figures, but if the Yankee is a good waiter, as this one seemed to be, he will doubtless get the article, say for $350.00, after which bargain completed, the Oriental will be ready to spend another tranquil hour in selling him a rug from Smyrna or a scarf from Syria.

Most of the streets of the city are narrow and tortuous, but there are more modern sections where broad thoroughfares and carriage drives abound. Here are the English and European shops, and the residences of the well-to-do foreigners in the city. The old native families, both Turkish and Armenian, inhabit the water front from the sea of Marmora to the Golden Horn, where their palaces leave off and the splendid dwellings of foreign ambassadors begin; and at this point the channel is crossed by the Galatia bridge, which introduces one to a colony composed of Levantines, and the scum of all Europe—perhaps the basest villains on the face of the earth.

Such in brief outline is Constantinople—a city marvelously full of interest to the observer of human nature or the student of human events, because here, as nowhere else in the world, the various states of Oriental and Occidental civilization, with all their dross and all their gems, crop up side by side, and may be intelligently compared—a spot where trade is affected by every wave that tosses on every sea, where thought is stirred by every brain that pulsates under any sky, where life is truly cosmopolitan.

THE FALL OF THE BYZANTINE EMPIRE.

Although the Turks had conquered all Thrace, although city after city had heard the clash of the Musselman's arms, and had been compelled to bow before his onward march, there was one city, the pride and glory of the Byzantine empire, that still remained unconquered. Constantinople, the Rome of the East, and capital of the empire, was the jewel that Mohammed II. most coveted. How to gain this jewel for his crown was his constant thought. It haunted him wherever he went. It interfered with his usual sleep. Long after midnight, when all his camp reposed in peaceful slumber, this restless spirit paced to and fro in his apartments, seeking to devise some means to reach his cherished end. One thing he had determined: he would win Constantinople or die. Such men seldom fail.

One thousand masons were commanded to erect at once a fortress on the European shore of the Bosphorus, known as Castle of Europe. As the work of this construction rapidly progressed, Constantine, the Byzantine emperor, sought by compromise, treaty and submission to avert the designs of the implacable Sultan, all to no avail. The Sultan did not want compromise; he wanted war, and any excuse was welcome. "Since then," despairingly wrote the emperor, "neither oaths, nor treaty, nor submission can secure peace, pursue your impious warfare. My trust is in God alone, and if it should please Him to modify your heart, I shall rejoice in the happy change. If he delivers the city into your hands, I submit without a murmur to His holy will; but until the Judge of the earth shall pronounce between us, it is my duty to live and die in the defense of my people."

To Mohammed this was a signal sound of strife; gigantic were the preparations. A foundry was established at Adrianople, and a cannon ordered to be made capable of battering down the strongest wall.

These instructions were well followed, and a gun produced of enormous dimensions, capable of sending a ball weighing 600 pounds over a mile. Boats were constructed, warriors enlisted, until the number in the army was swelled to nearly 250,000.

Battering rams were placed near the gates of St

Romanus, towers were moved on rollers to the ditch outside the city, from which ladders could be extended to the wall. The immense cannons were placed in position, and on the morning of the eighth of April, 1453, preparations were completed.

Nor during all these months were the inhabitants of the city inactive, yet the defense was weak. From the time the first dark clouds of danger had begun to threaten, thousands deserted their homes and firesides and left the city to the defense of the few. Finally, out of over 100,000 inhabitants only 6,000 could be found to take up arms and with the emperor repel the invaders, and these were stationed at the weakest points.

Day after day did the Turks attempt to enter the city, and as often were they repulsed by this Gideon's band.

The first assault was a failure, and the treasures of Constantinople lay still untouched by impious hands. Six weeks dragged slowly on—weeks of anxious suspense and hope, weeks, every day of which was filled with preparations. Reinforcements were received by the Turks. Three hundred boats were transported ten miles overland to the harbor in the dead of night.

More cannons were pointed towards walls already shattered. Mohammed had cause to believe that the city could not withstand another attack, and it was divinely revealed to him that the twenty-ninth of May should be the day of a second assault. On the eve of the twenty-ninth, as the sun sank to the western sky, it saw a sight weird

and strange. From the domes inside the city was reflected
its golden light, and flashing in the sun shone the polished
weapons of a restless army outside the wall. The sun went
down, the stars came out and shone upon a scene, weirder,
stranger still.

The Sultan strode among his men and told them of the
Paradise that waits for those who bravely fight and die. A
province would he give to him who first should scale
the city wall. He told them of rich treasures that would
all be theirs if victory they gained upon the morrow; and
not till midnight did he find his tent to indulge in a few
hours of fitful sleep.

From watch towers all along the wall, night guards
watched the Moslem hosts below. There was no sleep in
Constantinople that night. If we had wended our way
through the deserted streets to the church of St. Sophia, we
would have seen the Greek emperor, Constantine, ride up,
dismount, and, with his few chosen knights, enter the
magnificent portals, and, on bended knee, with head low
bowed before the images of the virgin and numerous saints,
in vain implore, in a fervent prayer, their mercy for safe
deliverance.

Before the altar, under dimly burning tapers he knelt.
Above him circled a gorgeous dome, which for centuries had
echoed with many supplications to the Almighty. Upon
the walls, hundreds of costly jewels reflected the low,
flickering rays, and as he thought that for the last time he
gazed upon these sacred walls, with bitter tears, his brave

heart sank within him. To-morrow his scepter would be wrested from him.

Ere the morrow's sun had set, the altar where he had knelt so many times would be defiled, and he who prayed there now would be no more. Fate thus whispered to the imperial head. But not without a struggle would he surrender the empire of his fathers, and walking out into the night again he ascended the tower to watch. Slowly the hours dragged on; all was still, save the muffled tread of soldiers outside the city, and, as the dawn approached, the watchfires grew less and less distinct and slowly sank to ashes.

Far in the east, a faint streak of grey announced the break of morn. A moment, and a dozen cannons volleyed forth with loud report. The calm was changed into a mighty storm. The thunders of battle furiously roared within and without. Loud rose commands of generals in the heart of bloody conflict. Clouds of dust and smoke overwhelmed women and children wandering the streets in a heart-rending search for a last refuge. What an awful vision of human ambition and revenge! Shrieks of the wounded, groans of the dying, wild exclamations, cheers and struggles of the living, awe-inspiring martial music rising here and there above the clash and clang of arms. Like a mighty whirlwind, on, on, towards St. Romanus' gate advance attacking thousands.

For a moment they waver; hand to hand in a death struggle they grapple with resisting Greeks. Back, slowly back, they force the few that struggle hardest; then, with a mighty, sudden onslaught, down the handful of Greeks that remain. Then arises, from two hundred thousand throats, the wild cry of victory. *Allah Ekber, Allah Ekber!* rends the air, and the Byzantine empire, in one brief day has fallen! The flickering light of the eastern Roman empire has been extinguished once for all! The faithful emperor, Constantine, was among the slain. All save a few of his brave soldiers died fighting at the gate. That night the setting sun beheld a different sight. No army lay encamped outside the city wall, but high over the ramparts floated an alien flag--the star and crescent of the Turks.

In the preceding pages I have endeavored to present the history, and portray as accurately as possible the customs of my native land.

As I pen these last few words my mind instinctively turns to my countrymen, zealous in the faith, constant to the right, the type of a fearless, honorable race.

Providence has so ordained that the peoples of earth should be divided into nations, the governments and laws of which are as diverse as the ideas peculiar to their originators. We may be united in civilization and common sympathies, but the patriot is ever proud and even inconsistently partial to that land which has given him birth.

Christianity is broader than any constitution, more effective than the most wise laws of men. Its kingdom is confined to no territory, has no limitations to its power, and its people stand firm on its first vital principles. We are all patriots of that kingdom, and it is not only loyalty to my country but loyalty to the broader, more glorious kingdom that prompts me to turn my purposes and energy to her welfare.

The light of morning already tints the eastern sky, but the mists still rising from man's own ignorance and superstition obscure the rays and hide the sun. When, rising over hill and valley with its glorious splendor, God's own light shines in the zenith of the heavens, the obscuring mists all cleared away, then, and not till then, will the soul of man be fully illumined and his destiny made clear.

www.ingramcontent.com/pod-product-compliance
Lightning Source LLC
Chambersburg PA
CBHW031937230426
43672CB00010B/1953